D0934438

37653013637676
Main NonFiction: 1st flr
796.334 CASCIO
Soccer U.S.A.

DN

CENTRAL ARKANSAS LIBRARY SYSTEM
LITTLE ROCK PUBLIC LIBRARY
700 LOUISIANA STREET
LITTLE ROCK, ARKANSAS 72201

Soccer U.S.A.

Chuck Cascio

Soccer U.S.A.

Robert B. Luce, Inc. Washington — New York

Copyright © 1975 by Chuck Cascio

All rights reserved, including the right to reproduce this book, or parts thereof, in any form, except for the inclusion of brief quotations in a review.

Cascio, Chuck.
  Soccer U. S. A.

  1. Soccer—United States.   I. Title.

GV944.U5C37   796.33'4'0973   75-11370
ISBN 0–88331–075–9

to those who sacrificed so others may write

76-4460
CENTRAL ARKANSAS LIBRARY SYSTEM
BOOKMOBILE DEPARTMENT
700 LOUISIANA
LITTLE ROCK, ARKANSAS

Contents

vii

1.   An Unsocial History of Soccer

In January of 1965 on the island of Chios in Greece, a Catholic priest strolled briskly through the streets toward the harbor. A slight breeze tugged at his cassock and his eyes focused straight ahead as he boarded a ship leaving the island. Suddenly, a shout arose from the crowd and the priest froze momentarily. He listened. A crescendo of shouts began swelling. He quickened his pace and attempted to hide among the other passengers on the boat. But it was too late. He'd been spotted.

A tangerine hit his neck and the juice trickled down soaking his white collar. Then an orange, followed by a tomato, and then another tangerine found their marks. Soon a shower of assorted fruit scattered the passengers while the priest tried to duck for shelter, whispering a prayer of thanks that he wasn't being hit by something a little more powerful than an impromptu fruit salad. You see, in the eyes of thousands of people on Chios, he had sinned most grievously. It was not that he had done something unpriestly, for in reality he wasn't a priest. He was Constantine Fatouros, a soccer official who had made a crucial call against the old home team earlier in the day and, after the game, in an attempt to escape the hostile home crowd, had disguised himself as a priest.

Unfortunately for Constantine, and for the other passengers who were also showered with fruit juice spray, he was discovered and made to pay a relatively mild price.

Meanwhile, in Yugoslavia, same month, same year, an interesting series of events took place. They began when referee Djordje Stanisic was forced into making a close call which, naturally, many spectators disagreed with. To Djordje's relief and surprise the crowd only expressed its anger with widespread booing. The relief was only temporary, however, for within minutes Djordje noticed some peculiar actions on the part of the soccer players, as members of both teams began scattering in all directions. It took Djordje only an instant to realize that the car horn he was hearing behind him had something to do with this strange activity. When he turned and saw the car bearing down on him from some twenty five yards away, Djordje ran too.

Like a stumble-footed matador avoiding the charging bull, Djordje avoided the car. Like a quarterback who has roamed out of the pocket and lost his helmet would dodge onrushing linemen, Djordje dodged the car. Like a prisoner praying before execution, Djordje prayed. And the car followed, narrowly missing him. Just when it seemed that fatigue would overcome him, a wonderful thing happened. Djordje heard a loud noise, and then a hissing sound. He heard the sounds three more times in rapid succession before he realized that all four of the car's tires had been punctured by gunshots. The police to the rescue? No, just a fan who happened to agree with Djordje's decision and didn't want to see him done away with—at least not until Djordje blew a call in the eyes of his savior. The fan put his gun away to the mixed reactions of the crowd.

Just a month earlier in Beirut, Lebanon, a soccer official had not faired as well as Djordje Stanisic. Then too there were gunshots after he made a controversial call. Unfortunately, in this case the shots were intended for the official and they hit him, causing serious injuries.

In Beirut the same day as the shooting but in a different game, a spectator attacked and hospitalized a soccer player after he scored a goal against the favored team.

Then there is the plight of one Vincente Feola of Brazil, who in 1966 became one of the most unpopular men in his country's history. The portly Feola was manager of Brazil's World Cup team in 1966 when the team shocked the world by being ousted from competition. Perennial champions, the Brazilian national team had been undefeated since 1964. Knowing that his countrymen would not take the loss lightly, Feola went into hiding outside Brazil. Thousands of furious and humiliated Brazilians hung Vincente in effigy and stoned his home, where his wife was being guarded by police.

When the furor subsided, Vincente slipped back into the country and kept himself out of the public eye. Just when it seemed Feola had nothing more to get used to than a lifetime of paranoia, an influenza epidemic swept through Brazil. The illness was so vile that it seemed only one name could fully communicate its heinous nature. So it became known as "grippe Feola," condemning Vincente to a lifetime of ignominy. Everyone who ached, grew feverish, and vomited would curse Feola while they suffered and surely still remember him today.

Medical experts say that when a person's adrenalin is stimulated he can do extraordinary things — lift cars, bend steel, run for miles. That soccer ranks extremely high in producing adrenalin was dramatically illustrated in London in May, 1969, at a game between West Ham United and visiting Stoke City. Mrs. Sheila West and her two sons (ages four and eight) were among some 26,000 West Ham fans watching their heroes battle to a scoreless tie. Mrs. West agreed with the popular view that the officiating by referee Tom Reynolds was inadequate, and when he blew the final whistle she made her displeasure clear by attacking him. Telling her kids something like, "Mommy will be back in a minute," West ran onto the field, tackled Reynolds and pummeled him with her fists as she did her best to meet the demands of the crowd which was screaming "We want a riot!"

Several minutes and five bobbies later, West was pulled off of Reynolds, who was not badly injured. In addition to winning the fight West won herself a night on the town with her husband who declared, "I'm proud of her," when informed of her day's activity.

And then there have been the mass misfortunes caused by frenzied crowd reactions during soccer games throughout the world.

June, 1964, Athens, Greece: 25,000 people believed the match they were watching was fixed. In protest, they set fire to the stadium.

Spring 1970: During World Cup tournament play El Salvador and Honduras battled fiercely in a hotly disputed game eventually won by El Salvador. Fans of the victors, euphoric over their win, couldn't resist rubbing it in and immediately began taunting Honduras' fans. Formal protests were exchanged by the two tiny countries, and less formal brawling broke out. Eventually, an all out war which lasted three days developed, leaving 3,000 dead and thousands more injured. Of course, the causes of the war went deeper than soccer, but it was the game that sparked the fuse. When writers write that "countries have gone to war over soccer," this is the war they mean.

May, 1964, Lima, Peru: The Peruvian national team met Argentina in pre-Olympic competition. At the height of action during a physically and emotionally draining game, referee Eduardo Pazo disallowed a crucial Peruvian goal. Immediately following the decision, several small groups of people seemed to be struck by the same idea at once — get the official.

Masses of people began moving in one direction down narrow aisles. A few pushes, a couple of kicks, a toe stepped on here and there, and angry punches were thrown. Within minutes, fighting had broken out and the field was overrun by stampeding spectators who soon forgot their initial reason for taking the field and began releasing their unbridled emotions on each other. Even the most innocent observers panicked and soon 45,000 became an uncontrollable rabble seeking escape by any means. People were trampled, beaten, knived, and shot. Others, in their attempts to flee, were suffocated by human congestion in the narrow exits.

Lima's morgues became so full the dead were placed on lawns. Police donned steel helmets and used tear gas to quell the rioting which spilled into the streets. When peace was finally restored, the soccer riots had claimed some 300 lives and left over 300 more people injured.

These examples are not meant to imply that the U.S. needs any more violence than it already has. They merely show the intensity the sport generates in foreign countries. Soccer's roots are deep and the stories of its beginnings are numerous and varied. Greeks, Romans,

Asians, Latin Americans and cavemen have all been credited with discovering something similar to soccer.

In parts of ancient Asia, a form of the game was played for very high stakes. Teams played as if their lives depended on it — for good reason. Winning sides were awarded assorted valuables and celebrated in grand fashion. Losers were sometimes executed or enslaved. Now that could make for some pretty furious play.

The Romans in particular make a claim to establishing the roots of soccer since, in the Roman heyday, they played a game called harpastum. This game was played in roughly the following manner: a ball was thrown into the air and everyone pushed, fought and kicked to get it beyond a pre-established point which served as a goal. It was popular among Roman soldiers during the occupation of England and they held an annual super-match at the town of Chester (named by the Romans) on Shrove Tuesday as part of the festivities prior to the fasting season. Brutality and out-and-out violence prevailed at this annual harpastum match until finally it was replaced by footraces. This, of course, dismayed the fans at Chester who, it seems, preferred the physical action of harpastum to the more genteel footrace. The game was eventually reinstated and Shrove Tuesday still brings the same all-out match by village residents.

But the Romans' claim to soccer is not all that convincing. Harpastum involved kicking as only part of all-out warfare. Besides, the word harpastum itself is Greek, indicating the Roman game was probably adapted from a Greek form.

When all arguments have been heard, it is the British, thanks to a hard-headed Dane and some fun-loving,

14

morbid English workers who have the best case for having started a game most closely resembling soccer today. In the process of digging at an old battle site, a skull, which one of the English workers promptly claimed once belonged to a Danish soldier (how he made that split second determination is one of the mysteries of the game), was uncovered. With that idea in mind, one of the workers kicked the bloody thing out of bitterness. It rolled to a stop in front of a fellow worker who quickly picked up the idea and put his best foot into it. The activity caught on and before long the workers were chasing after the skull in an effort to get more kicks in before the skull became pieces of skull.

A group of boys was watching the workers at play and, quick to recognize fun when they saw it, wanted to join in. Unfortunately, the skull was being steadily chipped away by the men's furious kicking, so one ingenious young chap suggested using something more durable, like an inflated cow bladder. That idea proved popular with everyone since cow bladders were somewhat easier to come by than human skulls. They were also rounder, bounced more, hurt less, rolled farther, and were harder to keep up with.

The game caught on and neighboring townspeople enthusiastically made it part of their regular exercising routine. Soon, informal groups of players began to form in towns to challenge other groups. Yards of ale were frequently wagered as teams met and began kicking cow bladders and each other apart. Next in the progression came towns challenging other towns, and it was not uncommon for hundreds of people to join in the festivities. Inter-town matches began with the bladder being placed at a point equidistant from both towns. Then

Despite changes in the game over the years, soccer still has its highly physical side. *Washington Diplomats photos.*

the townfolk started kicking. The losing team was the team winding up with the bladder being kicked into its town. Losers were expected to entertain their victorious guests, and the festivities were frequently more strenuous still.

In 1365 Edward III of England prohibited the game for military reasons. His troops, it seems, were equally concerned with victory on the soccer "pitch" and victory on the battle field, and the two just didn't mix in the king's mind. Besides, if the king's soldiers were going to be injured, he wanted them injured in military, not soccer combat.

It didn't work. In fact, banning the game only fueled its popularity. Towns would break out a bladder (actually, it was evolving into a more sophisticated looking type of ball) and play anyway, and since the king's men were enthusiastic participants, the townspeople were rarely stopped from playing. Still the rulers tried — Richard II, Henry IV, Henry VIII and Elizabeth I all attempted to deflate enthusiasm for the game, but soccer only became more firmly entrenched in British hearts. Even Shakespeare found occasion to refer to the game of the people in his *Comedy of Errors,* Act II:

> "Am I so round with you as you with me
> That like a football you spurn me thus?
> You spurn me here and will spurn me hither;
> If I last in this service you must case me in leather."

By the nineteenth century soccer was a natural, accepted part of English life. As the Empire spread, so spread the game, and it was soccer that survived though the Empire crumbled. Anywhere that soccer was introduced, organized groups had a representative team.

18

There were town teams, army teams, church teams and others. By 1900 the sport was part of Olympic competition. Today it is the most widely played game in the world.

The name of the game is soccer. Its appeal, while not always healthy, is immense. Because it is truly a world sport, in most countries soccer breeds excitement that is often uncontrollable. In some cities moats complete with drawbridges have been constructed around soccer stadiums to keep gate crashers out during matches. And while crowd reactions following a loss have often been deplorable, the elation of the masses following victories has touched off some of sport's most memorable celebrations.

Perhaps no sports victory brings the same kind of pride that winning soccer's World Cup brings. True, the U.S. has seen half a million people take over Pittsburgh following the Steelers' Super Bowl IX victory. Met fans made their marks in Shea Stadium by stuffing their pockets with turf ripped from the field when the Mets won their first "World" Championship in 1969. Still, the quotation marks around the word "world" make the celebrations for sports like football, baseball, basketball and hockey a little false.

You don't see the Los Angeles Rams or Houston Oilers playing teams from Rome or Madrid for a world championship in football. There are probably no foreign countries (unless you consider Canada foreign, but then the U.S. and Canada don't square off either) that can afford to field professional football teams; so the U.S. champ is "world" champ by default. Making the situation more ridiculous is the World Football League, which includes teams only within the U.S., claims a "World" Bowl Champion, but doesn't even compete against the

National Football League in its own country.

Baseball determines its "world" champions from teams strictly within the U.S.A. (except Montreal). No formal money-on-the line challenges are made to teams from Japan, South America, Central America or the Philippines to compete for a more complete world title, though the game is followed with enthusiasm equal to or surpassing that expressed in the U.S. Yet baseball calls its championhip games the World Series.

No teams from the National Basketball Association play for championships outside the U.S. either, yet the annual champion is proclaimed the best in the world. In reality, until the NBA and the American Basketball Association get together for a playoff, there's no way even of determining which league has the best team in the country.

No such problem exists with soccer, the world's most widely played sport. When a country wins the World Cup it has won a tournament involving teams from all over the globe. So the celebrations and distinctions bestowed on members of the victorious teams are lavish indeed.

2.   International Warfare

The World Cup games are more than games to competing teams, especially those teams that are among the final sixteen after early eliminations. The contests become part of a national movement, a country rallying behind a team involved in a war fought with feet and a ball instead of bullets and bombs. The United States has had only two significant moments in World Cup play — in the first World Cup competition in 1930 and again in 1950. With little tradition in soccer, the American public has not experienced the nationalistic fervor felt by the rest of the world over the contests. But as professional soccer grows in the U.S., the World Cup games will become a focal point of that growth and Americans will certainly become at least as involved as other nations. People will be drawn by the games because they are played by professional competititors. They represent the best of the country's soccer players. These are men who, in most cases, must produce on the field in order to eat at home. The World Cup games will let us see how we stack up against the rest of the world's pros — and there's the attraction.

The original World Cup trophy was a greatly cherished hunk of metal, a winged gold figure standing merely 12 inches tall. Named after Jules Rimet, the French president of the Federation of International Football Associations (FIFA), soccer's international ruling body, the trophy was coveted for symbolic rather than economic reasons. During World War II, German soldiers searched all over Italy for the trophy but were unable to find it. It seems the Italians had anticipated such a hunt and, showing a flair for the imaginative, shuffled the precious cargo to safety in Switzerland. When the war ended and competition resumed in 1950, the Italians recovered the trophy and produced it safe and-a sound-a.

Perhaps an incident in England in 1966 best illustrates the symbolic value of the Cup itself. The trophy was on display in Central Hall in London, where the 1966 games were held. Next to the trophy was a set of stamps valued at some $8 million. Thieves, obviously soccer fans, broke into the Hall and stole the trophy but left the stamps untouched. The theft precipitated a search that Sherlock Holmes would have been proud of and the Rimet Cup was recovered to the relief of everyone, especially British officials who were beginning to feel some international heat.

The World Cup competition in 1978 will provide a good idea of exactly how much the U.S. has progressed in soccer. The success or failure of the U.S. team will play a large part in determining if public interest in soccer increases or decreases. Teams in the United States have stepped up their competition against foreign countries in recent years with only modest success.

Taking direct aim on 1978 competition, the U.S. now has a national team which trains and plays together periodically, something the country has never had before. As Walter Bahr, a member of the 1950 U.S. World Cup team recalls, "We didn't have any practices together, we had just played a lot against international competition together. Following World War II a lot of foreign teams toured the country, and I guess I played over 150 games against them. We played in Scotland in front of 108,000 fans without ever practicing and got clobbered 6-0."

The fact that the present U.S. team practices and plays together should help. However, some early scores indicate that the U.S. is far from ready to frighten many first-line national teams. In the spring of 1975 the national team played in Italy and Poland, and the results were disheartening. Poland pasted the U.S. 7-0, but then, Poland is the third best soccer team on earth. Italy, the fifth best on earth, increased the humiliation to 10-0. The Polish olympic team, gold medal winners in 1972, also beat the U.S. national team 3-0, and an Italian club team triumphed 2-1.

Prior to the European trip, the U.S. national team played Mexico home-and-home. The first game, played in Mexico, was a 3-0 defeat for the U.S., and the second, played in Dallas three days later, was a 1-0 defeat.

With losses like those, the U.S. team must look for small pieces of encouragement. For example, chalk the beatings up to experience, particularly the European affairs, and try to learn from them. Kyle Rote Jr., a member of the U.S. team and the biggest American name in the game, does just that. Rote, an intense player and a student of the game who knows he has a lot to learn, keeps notes on all of his games. While he feels "it would have been better to play Switzerland, Norway or Austria or Greece, instead of Poland and Italy, to get the European flavor without taking on top teams right away," he kept his trusty notebook with him and "learned a lot."

"Just to see the way these teams used their players was valuable," says Rote. "Italy uses four fullbacks and a sweeper. Two of the fullbacks are wing fullbacks with highly developed offensive skills, so that means they have the ability to leave their defensive positions and score. That puts tremendous pressure on the defensive team. Two of the goals by Italy's Roca came from a non-attacking position, but he was so fast he took off downfield and scored."

As Rote talks about the foreign players, he expresses an admiration bordering on awe. He reads his notes quietly, ponders them and then continues his remarks casually, yet with a "you have to see it to believe it" tone.

"The Italian center forward hardly ran at all," Rote recalls. "He was always in good position, never near the sidelines. He restricted his running to straight line running and acted more or less like a traffic cop."

"Poland," he says after another reflective pause, "Poland just had great finishing skills. Anything near the penalty circle always resulted in a close shot on goal. Any slightly loose ball and the forwards pounced on it. And the Poles had a method of tackling that I still can't figure out. Here in the U.S. we learn the one-leg slide tackle where you slide and try to take the ball away with your lead leg and then pull the other leg through. The Poles have developed the slide tackle where, if the lead leg misses, they get you with the trailing leg.

"Then there was the passing in Europe. Here, we pass to space. In other words, we try to anticipate where the man we want to pass to will meet up with the ball and then we pass to that spot. Over there, because players can run as fast with the ball as without it, they pass to the man's feet. They can pick up the dribble that quick, without breaking stride."

Rote, who compares playing in Europe with participating in a marathon run — "You wonder if all the pain is worth it" — admits he thought at times, "What in the world am I doing here?" Yet, his natural competitiveness already has him thinking about how the national team could improve its play against the Europeans, should they meet again.

"If you're attacking, you don't get as tired as when you're chasing" he says, prefacing a strategy he feels the U.S. should try. "We've got to allow ourselves the right to fail as long as we're playing supportively and aggressively. The problem we had in Europe was that we weren't willing to risk leaving our men to help out a teammate on offense because of the man-to-man defense we played. The defense prohibited supportive runs; we can't allow it to do that.

"For example, if a teammate steals the ball twenty yards downfield and I'm guarding their center half, I should go to a supportive position for my teammate. However, if I go, it means leaving my opponent open and if my teammate loses the ball, my man is all alone."

So, though Rote wouldn't approve of the language, he's damned if he does and damned if he doesn't. If he goes to aid his teammate, he risks the embarrassment of leaving his man all alone, not to mention the wrath of the coach if the man should score. If he doesn't help out, his teammate stands around waiting for a European to steal the ball back, which will occur in a matter of seconds. Rote would seem to have a point. Playing tight man-to-man, the team allowed 22 goals in Europe and scored only one. Perhaps they could learn from the old American

25

football axiom: "The best defense is a strong offense."

Rote also noticed, particularly against Poland, more concern for accuracy in shots taken rather than sheer power of the shots. "They beat our goalkeepers with placement, not power. They didn't blast shots, but they used good technique and finesse to make sure every shot was around the goal." That's the kind of pressure that eventually causes a goalkeeper to crumble.

Coaching problems have also slowed the progress of the U.S. national team. In a big push to field a creditable team for the 1978 World Cup eliminations, the United States Soccer Federation (USSF) persuaded Dettmar Cramer of Germany to become the first fulltime U.S. national coach in July, 1974. Cramer, a Vince Lombardi type — shorter, perhaps, but with the same kind of hard work philosophy — came to the U.S. with an impressive background and an equally impressive plan of action.

Cramer brought 41 years of soccer experience as a player and a coach with him, including 17 years as the national association coach of the German Football Association, 10 years as assistant coach of the German Olympic and World Cup teams, and head coach of the 1964 Japanese Olympic team. In addition, Cramer was a master teacher of the game, having collaborated on several instructional soccer books and films.

After some initial doubts, Cramer agreed to coach the U.S. national team for four years at $50,000 per year. By January, 1975, after coaching the U.S. team to two losses against Mexico, his only two games as coach, he had left the U.S. to return to Germany and coach the perennially powerful Bayern-Munich club, which was suffering an uncharactaristically poor season. It seems Cramer had never signed a USSF contract, working under a verbal agreement while contract details were being ironed out. As time passed, Cramer was drawn to, and opted for, Bayern-Munich's more attractive offer.

Cramer's abrupt walkout was surprising and disappointing since he had begun to lay the groundwork for success. Cramer had given the U.S. some small hope for 1978 because of his background and also because he was charged with reorganizing the national teams — World Cup, Olympic, and National Junior Team (age 19 and under) — from grassroots on up. He had no affiliation with any American clubs, so he could concentrate completely on his national tasks.

What's more, he appeared to welcome the challenge. In the September, 1974 issue of *Soccer Monthly,* a magazine sponsored by the USSF, Cramer outlined his intentions in an article:

"I have a job at hand, and I will do everything within my power to finish it successfully. However, I am not a superman; I cannot create miracles. Good things take time, and soccer is a team game. Team spirit and teamwork are the prerequisites of success. No man can do it all by himself. . . . At the present moment only one thing is crystal clear: We will try to qualify for the 1978 World Cup in Argentina."

In his brief tenure as coach, Cramer travelled around the U.S. speaking of the need to develop American coaches who, in turn, would develop American talent. He referred to certain foreign players in America's professional ranks as "European phonies", and indicated that someday they would be replaced by the real, homegrown American product. He spouted variations on clichés like, "My job is to make the impossible possible, to try the untried," when talking about his construction work.

27

Announcement of his agreement to coach the U.S. had been greeted with unbridled enthusiasm in national soccer circles, and in some U.S. cities groups of Cramer supporters called "Dettmar's Disciples" were formed.

Cramer's oratory and whirlwind style slowed noticably when the club from Deutschland pulled at his heartstrings — and pursestrings. Bayern-Munich, 1974 European Cup Champions, had placed seven men on the 22 man German National squad which won the 1974 World Cup. Franz Beckenbauer, captain of Germany's national team and the head of Bayern-Munich, asked club officials to seek Cramer after former coach, Udo Lattek, was dumped. What Franz wants, Franz gets, so Bayern-Munich went after Cramer with the equivalent of a $100,000 per year contract.

Cramer, who often admitted to being "sensitive," became downright moved by the offer. In truth, he had always harbored some reservations about leaving his family in Germany and homesickness combined with money is a hard combination to ignore. It has been known to make commitments take a back seat.

The USSF responded to the shock by launching a $10 million suit against Cramer and Bayern-Munich. However, the lack of a signed contrct and an increasing attitude of "who wants a coach who doesn't want us?" resulted in the USSF dropping the suit by late February, 1975.

Cramer, whose wardrobe reportedly consists mainly of the sweatsuits he coaches in, should not be viewed completely as a traitor. True, he didn't exhibit the long range tenacity he indicated he would. But he was faced with a huge organizational task in a country hoping to take giant steps in a relatively short period of time.

Working without a firm signed contract is not the most secure situation, no matter how good the employer's intentions, and when an organized, established club like Bayern-Munich waved stability in Cramer's face, he did the natural though perhaps not the most ethical thing and accepted. He left the U.S. national team high and dry and the USSF understandably red-faced — with embarrassment and anger. To further the embarrassment, Bayern-Munich went on to win the European Cup in 1975 under Cramer's supervision.

The problems facing the national team were compounded by the USSF's failure to name a fulltime national team coach immediately following Cramer's departure. Instead, Al Miller, coach of the NASL's Philadelphia Atoms and Cramer's assistant national coach, was named interim coach. The American-born Miller, a popular choice, was put in the unenviable position of splitting his time between his own team and the national team. By the summer of 1975, after Miller had accompanied the national team to the slaughters in Italy and Poland in the spring, Manny Schellscheidt, coach of the NASL's Hartford Bicentennial, was preparing to replace Miller as interim coach. When Poland played the U.S. in Seattle on June 24, 1975, the Schellscheidt coached team lost 4-0.

The unstable coaching situation, plus difficulties in arranging a practice site and date suitable to all national team members, plus being inadequately prepared for World Class opponents, has slightly tainted the honor of being on the team. Some players can't always leave their fulltime jobs to make trips and practice or play with the team. Bob Rigby, goalkeeper for the Philadelphia Atoms and a member of the national team, seven months after

Cramer's pullout gave some indication of the difficulties facing the national team movement:

"A fulltime coach must be named so he can pick a team. The big decision is, will he be American or foreign? Whatever the decision, it should be made soon.

"Cramer stressed a complete team idea where everyone got involved in the competition. We saw some fantastic results in a couple of months with him, but it would have taken more time to really see complete results. He wasn't here long enough to tell how far he'd have taken us.

"But when you come right down to it, the American thing isn't as important as making a living. You have to look out for yourself first, so I'm working on a deal to play on a European club on loan from the Atoms. If the national team wants me, they'll fly me in. If not, that's okay too."

The blame for the dwindling morale of the U.S. national team lies heavily with the USSF, and pro team officials, as well as members of the media who cover soccer pound away at the organization with little effect. They point to the lack of coordination and the absence of adequate publicity and public relations as the major flaws of the organization. The bungling of the Cramer situation did little to inspire confidence in the Federation, and if the national team does begin to improve, it may be in spite of the USSF rather than because of it.

Despite the difficulties the U.S. national team faces, soccer people in the country are guardedly optimistic about future U.S. involvement in World .Cup play. Dennis Viollet, coach of the NASL's Washington Diplomats who played for England in a 1966 World Cup qualifying round game, says in his clipped British accent,

"The World Cup fervor will catch on in the United States as the U.S. team goes down the road to the World Cup. And I'll tell you what else — and this is a virtual certainty — as soon as FIFA feels the U.S. can draw the kinds of crowds needed to cover the costs of hosting the games, the U.S. will be the host country. When that happens, since the host country automatically qualifies as one of the 16 finalists, see how people react. You can bet your last nickel that the U.S. will get the games just as soon as FIFA feels it's ready for them."

When the coaching difficulties are corrected and the U.S. has matured soccer-wise, American businessmen, tops at smelling out a buck-making opportunity, will push hard for the games. The sources of income are endless — gate receipts, closed circuit television, concessions, a million tie-in possibilities, not to mention the general economic boom to local commerce in whichever city gets the games. Of course, there are risks. Political turmoil, crazed crowds and the possibility of international "incidents" are always present during World Cup competition. It's a good thing Henry Kissinger's a soccer fan — he may be needed if and when the games come to the U.S.

The intensity of World Cup games belies the fact that the games have only been held 10 times. In fact, the games were initially snubbed by many soccer-playing nations. World Cup play began in 1930 mainly because the Olympics did not allow international competition on a professional level. Since soccer is the national sport of so many nations, countries were considerably upset that they were represented by amateurs in world competition while their best soccer talent could not be displayed. So soccer's world governing body, FIFA, met in 1928 and came up with the World Cup idea, scheduling play for 1930 and every four years thereafter. FIFA decreed Uruguay, winner of the 1924 and 1928 Olympic soccer gold medals, as host nation. But the whole World Cup idea almost never made it off the ground.

1930

World Cup play always seems to be surrounded by some kind of off-field conflict, and the first World Cup was no exception. Uruguayans were understandably proud to host the 1930 World Cup play since the games coincided with their centennial celebrations and since they would have the opportunity to show the world their superiority on the professional level of soccer just as they had done on the amateur level. Many European countries, notably Italy and England, acted as if traveling to South America for World Cup play would have the same effect as vacationing in a leper colony, and they refused to cross the Atlantic to play. In reality, the Europeans seemed bothered by the age-old problem of who would officiate, so rather than put their professional reputations on the line in a potentially hostile environment, they stayed home and missed the fun.

Squabbles over rules, balls, fan activity and playing and living conditions abounded, but the games went on though only 13 teams competed, all but five (France, Rumania, Yugoslavia, Belgium and the United States) from South America. Surprisingly, the United States entry fared well against the limited competition, defeating Belgium and Paraguay by 3-0 scores, before being eliminated by Mexico.

Not surprisingly, the final game was all South American, pitting Argentina against Uruguay. It also came as no surprise that police ringed the playing field as thousands of Uruguayans watched their national team win the first World Cup 4-2.

1934

In 1934 it was a different story altogether. Italy wanted to host the World Cup and Italian officials let FIFA know it. The Italians saw it as a chance to display their growing might, symbolically at least, with a win on the soccer field. After eight congresses, FIFA decided Italy had a deal which couldn't be refused. In all, 32 countries decided to compete, but among the missing were Argentina and World Cup holder Uruguay, which showed it too knew how to snub its nose. The U.S. was Italy's first round opponent and the Italians outclassed the Americans 7-1.

Italy showed fascist tendencies on the soccer field, with aggressive play by exceptionally strong men in perfect physical condition. The Italians' toughest two games came against Spain in Florence. In the first contest the two teams literally battled to a 1-1 tie in a game which cost Spain seven players through injuries. The next day, Spain's remaining players valiantly staved off the brutal Italians, who had come up with four new faces on the team, but the hobbled Spaniards eventually succumbed 1-0. After a two-day rest, Italy continued its tough-guy play to defeat a team of very large Austrians 1-0, and qualify for the final against Czechoslovakia.

How do you beat an Italian in Rome? The spunky Czechs came within eight minutes of supplying the answer. Holding tenaciously to a 1-0 lead, the Czechs were just eight minutes away from ruining the antipasto of Italians all over the country, when an Italian shot slithered by the Czech goalkeeper to tie the score and send the game into overtime. Revived and rejuvenated by the cheers (and threats) of the mob of 55,000, the Italians overpowered the Czechs in overtime and won 2-1, which was probably best for all involved.

1938

By the third World Cup, the idea of the competition was spreading and 36 countries entered play. The games were held in France in honor of Jules Rimet and the third World Cup games were appropriately wild affairs with all but two of the 18 first round matches going into overtime.

The Italian team, determined to capture its second straight World Cup, was well prepared for the 1938 games. Keeping its aggressive style and stingy defense, it added a more potent striking force to boost its scoring punch. But Brazil, years later to become the scourge of world soccer, was making a lot of noise throughout France with a strong team led by "Black Diamond" Leonidas. However, in one of the great mysteries of World Cup play, when Brazil and Italy met in the semifinal, Leonidas did not play. The Brazilians claimed they were saving their star, who had scored three times in the first half and once in overtime against Poland, for the finals. That bit of illogic backfired, predictably, as Brazil lost to Italy.

Italy, Olympic soccer champ in 1936, dominated Hungary in the World Cup final, winning 4-2 to capture its second straight World Cup title and gain undisputed claim to World Soccer Champion, pro and amateur.

1938-1950

The violence of international soccer paled in

comparison with the violence of international warfare, and the games were not held during the war years. By 1950, when World Cup play resumed in Brazil, general good feeling prevailed.

1950

The U.S. had flexed its military muscles during World War II and it sent a team to Brazil to flex its soccer muscles, an idea which drew chuckles from the rest of the world and guffaws from the few Americans who knew the game. Adding to the already seemingly impossible task for the U.S. team was the fact that it was placed in the same group as England, who finally saw fit to enter the games, and Spain. It looked like another early trip home for the Americans, especially when the U.S. lost to Spain 3-1.

Prior to the match against America in Belo Horizonte, proud England with centuries of soccer tradition, ho-hummed at the thought of playing the U.S. But 20,000 people watched in uncharacteristic silence as the Americans scraped, hustled, and, yes, lucked their way to a 1-0 upset. The only goal was scored on a classic header by Joe Gaetjens on an assist by Walter Bahr, now the head soccer coach at Penn State. Meanwhile, the English team watched its own shots float wide, glance off the crossbar, or hit the post. In disbelief, London newspapers questioned the 0-1 score, thinking it a misprint for 10-1. Some cynics tried to detract from the U.S. victory by pointing out that Gaetjens was born in Haiti, but that's what the old U.S. is all about, and deep down they knew it.

Just about the only place in the world not rocked by the result was the U.S., where people who heard about the victory said something like, "Really? How'd the Dodgers do today?"

In its next game the American team came crashing back into reality. Chile was hot and thrashed the U.S. 5-2.

Brazil emerged as the power of the games, combining for 13 goals against Sweden and Spain while yielding only two. The host country went into its final game against Uruguay a decided favorite. In Rio, 200,000 people stuffed themselves into Maracana Stadium to witness a much more challenging contest for the Brazilian team than expected. The rude Uruguayans yielded the first goal but then tightened on defense, got the offense in gear and scored twice to upset the Brazilians and maintain their record of never having lost in World Cup play.

1954

A new soccer force was born in the early fifties in Hungary, which won the 1952 Olympics and was building its reputation before the 1954 World Cup games by drubbing all comers, including England twice, in 1953. Hungary thus became the first foreign team to beat England in England. By 1954, when teams arived to compete for the World Cup in Switzerland, Hungary was the favorite to win the Rimet trophy.

Hungary set out early to live up to its reputation and did so by pummeling a German team 8-3. What Hungary did not know was that the Germans had played with substitutes, knowing they could afford a loss at that particular time without being eliminated from the games.

Then, in perhaps the most violent of all World Cup games, Hungary played Brazil in Bern. Insults, accusations, questionable officiating and a little soccer led to a 4-2 Hungarian victory. Punches were exchanged freely and often and eventually led to a locker room brawl. The young Brazilians screamed they were robbed, but to no avail.

Hungary followed the Brazilian Brawl with a 4-2 win over Uruguay, its first loss ever in World Cup competition, and faced the same German team it had demolished earlier, in the finals.

Only it wasn't the same German team. This time Germany played its regulars, not its reserves, and the overconfident Hungarians were upset 3-2.

1958

Heeere's Pelé! (known to his parents as Edson Arantes do Nascimento).

His name and tales of his talent have spread throughout the world, making him a legend. Barely civilized African tribes that play their soccer with human skulls supposedly shout "Pelé!" as they play. He's now the wealthiest athlete ever, but in 1958 he was just introducing himself to world soccer.

By age 17 Pelé had honed his soccer playing skills to the point where he was ready to travel to Sweden with the Brazilian national team to compete for the 1958 World Cup. It was in Sweden that young Pelé began making fans even of his dazzled opponents.

But even with Pelé, the road to the World Cup was not easy for Brazil. Fifty three countries had entered competition, and when the final 16 reached Sweden, the host country was a slight favorite over the rest of the pack. Indeed, Sweden was impressive as it rolled its way into the finals, but Pelé was drawing attention to Brazil by scoring the winning goal against Wales and booting in three goals in a 5-2 semifinal win over France.

It is not good copy for a legend-in-the-works to fail, and Pelé didn't. He gave glimpses of the superstar he would soon become, scoring once and helping Brazil to a 5-2 victory over Sweden, giving Brazil its first World Cup championship.

1962

Tragedy marred the 1962 World Cup games in Chile when the host country was devastated by an earthquake. The games were held anyway as Chileans tried to pull their lives together. The games themselves were tinged with slurs and fistfighting, very nearly making the actual play itself seem secondary to the violence.

The Chilean team, emotionally charged by events and the home crowd, played very physical soccer in defeating Yugoslavia, Switzerland and Italy. The Italians and Chileans mixed hot blood with hot words, resulting in some hot kicking and punching battles. Chile won the battles and the game, 2-0, and moved into the semifinal round against Brazil.

Brazil, with Pelé a 21-year-old veteran, was the early favorite to win its second straight World Cup. But the Brazilians, Pele included, seemed to be off their game and were lucky enough to win while playing lethargically.

Against Chile, the Brazilians were finally booted out of their trance-like state in a game where every other kick seemed to be aimed at a knee or some other vital area. Brazil did manage to kick four (soccer) balls into the goal while Chile could manage only two, ending Chile's crusade and setting the stage for a final pitting Brazil against Czechoslovakia.

In the final, Brazil, playing without the injured Pelé, lapsed back into lethargy long enough to allow the surprising Czechs to score first. Gradually Brazil regrouped, however, and rallied is somnambulent offense, eventually winning its second straight championship, 3-1.

1966

In this, the eighth World Cup, soccer burst upon the international scene with more intensity than ever before. Even in the United States millions of people followed the games and tuned in the final match on television, giving birth to the idea that perhaps the game just might catch on in the States

The games were played in England, and the host country at long last played World Cup soccer it did not have to be ashamed of. In fact, England won it all in a glamorous finale at Wembley Field before 97,000, including Queen Elizabeth and the Duke of Edinburgh.

Drama, physical play and surprise characterized the 1966 games. Not even the heroics of Pelé could rouse Brazil, and the aging, two-time champions fell unexpectedly to Portugal, losing their chance to compete in the quarterfinals. North Korea caused problems for members of the Italian team by defeating them 1-0, making many Italian players afraid to return home and face their angry countrymen. Those who did wished they hadn't as they were greeted with shouts which, politely translated, taunted, "You have disgraced Italy!" Edmondo Fabbri, the Italian manager, was fired immediately following the loss, and ten frightened and disappointed Italian players blamed team physician Dr. Fino Fini for the upset, resulting in a full-scale investigation by the Italian Soccer Federation.

England defeated Argentina in a quarterfinal match

Bob Rigby, a goal keeper for the U.S. national team, saves one . . .
Photo by Steve Hammond.

And misses one. . . . *Photo by Dennis Mallon.*

that, because of verbal assaults such as Britons calling the South Americans "animals" and worse, became a combination of Greco-Roman wrestling, savate and soccer. Meanwhile, West Germany achieved World Cup final play for the first time through cautious, mechanical play, defeating the Soviet Union along the way 2-1.

The finals, pitting proud England against West Germany, provided modern soccer with worldwide media coverage which, even in the United States, was at an all-time high. Mother England responded by putting on a gala performance.

The game itself was one of soccer history's finest. Prior to the end of regulation play, Englishmen had already begun celebrating. Their heroes had a 2-1 lead with one minute to play. The Germans, however, synchronized their play, charged a loose ball close to England's goal and booted it in to tie the game. Exhausted by the physical and emotional strain of a 2-2 tie at the end of regulation time, the members of both teams stretched out on the soggy field for some rest prior to the overtime.

It's doubtful that many of the half billion people around the world watching the game moved from their television sets at that point. The question was, can England recover from the fatigue and loss of momentum to satisfy the home crowd? An English player named Geoff Hurst took it upon himself to provide the positive answer. Hurst rallied himself and his teammates during overtime, kicking in two goals and leading England to a 4-2 victory.

The victory was followed by London's largest celebration since the end of World War II. Fire engines lined the streets and kept their sirens blaring and lights flashing throughout the night. British newspapers showed their pride on front pages in their biggest boldest types with headlines like "Golden Glory", "England, Lovely England", and "On Top of the World".

The British government even issued a stamp bearing a picture of the Cup and the proud boast "England Winners". The stamp was a smash — over 144,000 were sold in the first half hour they were available.

The excitement, pomp and money generated by the 1966 World Cup games did not go unnoticed in the U.S.A. These were the games that led to the birth of not just one, but three professional soccer leagues, financed by some of America's wealthiest sports figures.

1970

Because of the huge amount of worldwide attention drawn to the 1966 World Cup games, all media eyes were focused on Mexico for the 1970 games. High altitude and high temperatures drained many players, but World Cup competition has a way of expanding lungs just a little bit farther than normal, and the teams played as intensely as ever.

As usual, the intense competition led to tension and animosity. Mexican President Gustavo Diaz Ordaz set a hostile tone for the games during opening ceremonies when he handed the Mexican flag to his team and told them, "Play, as they say, until death to win." That's pressure.

It was death, indeed, for four people who were killed in a fire begun over a World Cup dispute. Another death occurred when, after Mexico defeated El Salvador, a fan casually said, "Mexico has nothing to be proud of because that Central American team was a lemon." He was shot.

From the start of play in Mexico, people were

looking forward to the contest between Brazil, winner in 1958 and 1962, and England, winner in 1966. The two teams were grouped in the same division and it was correctly assumed that they would meet for their group's championship and advancement to the semifinals. Pride was at stake for both teams — Brazil was looking for its third cup, which would allow it to retire the Rimet trophy, while England was out to prove that the 1966 championship truly indicated the way Britons played soccer.

Both teams were faced with personal obstacles to overcome. Brazil went into the games with a novice manager; England was bothered by hostile crowds and the equally hostile weather conditions. But when the teams met, they disappointed no one, including 21,500 U.S. fans in Madison Square Garden and its Felt Forum who paid anywhere from $5.00 to $12.50 per ticket to watch the game on closed circuit television. They saw quite a contest.

England played aggressive soccer for much of the game and eventually began to wear down. Brazil kept eliminating England's scoring opportunities, counting on fatigue to wilt the Britons. It did, and then Brazil seized the offensive, and won the match 1-0.

The well-rounded Brazilian team met the defense-oriented Italians in the finals. The winner of the game would also become the proud possessor of the Rimet trophy since both countries had won twice previously and a third victory would retire the cup. Blistering the Italian defense with goals by four different players, including Pelé, while yielding only one, Brazil laid permanent claim to the Rimet trophy. It seemed only fitting, since Brazil had the world's greatest player and a well-balanced team.

Munich's Olympic Stadium was the site for the 1974 World. Cup games, a frequently criticized series of contests. The problem, it seems, was that many of the teams turned defensive, protecting their own goal and waiting for their opponent to make a mistake before taking the offensive. Teams like Haiti, Australia, Zaire and Bulgaria made the final sixteen, and they were considered weak by traditional World Cup standards. Also dampening the traditional excitement was the fact that Pelé had retired and would not be playing for the Brazilians.

There were high points, to be sure. Holland, a country whose greatest players were playing for club teams in other parts of the world, lured them back for a run at the World Cup. Most notable among the returning Dutchmen was Johann Cruyff, who had been playing for Barcelona in Spain. He was purchased by the Spanish team for the equivalent of $3 million from the Dutch team Ajax. Cruyff's specialty was scoring goals, and he was a key to Holland's version of "total football," a type of play where everyone on the team helps push downfield. Total football was a relief to many fans who were bored by the defensive minded play of the other teams. The concept showed results as Holland scored 24 goals in six games leading up to the quarterfinals.

West Germany, host team, originator of the concept of total football, and winner of the European Champions Cup, was the early favorite to win the new World Cup. Tension was at its highest when West Germany met East Germany in a division game in Hamburg on June 22. In that struggle, which obviously was taken as more than a World Cup soccer game, the East Germans squelched the total soccer concept by winning 1-0. But though West Germany lost that particular battle, they made up for it by winning the war.

West Germany played Holland in the final match, a contest that promised more excitement than it actually produced. The Dutchmen played uninspired soccer, though 30,000 Dutch fans were there, and their offense never really developed. Cruyff did not explode as expected, and the West Germans outplayed Holland to come up with a 2-1 World Cup victory.

1978

A U.S. World Cup? Not a chance. In fact, if the U.S. team even makes a semi-serious run at the quarterfinals it will be a definite boost to soccer morale in the U.S. If the team does not reach the final 16, American soccer should not by any means be written off as an international failure. The Americanization process has been slow, even in the last decade when the sport finally reached somewhat legitimate professional status.

Greg Myers, coach of the Miami Toros of the NASL, feels that the importance of the 1978 World Cup games to American soccer has been overemphasized by some. "There are dreamers in this country who say we must win the World Cup in '78 to prove ourselves," Myers says. "But we won't win it, and so what if we don't? Soccer won't die because of it. We'll be back in '82 and '86 and one of these years the U.S. will be there to win it. We can't afford to go too fast; we'll make it eventually. The game is already coming along faster than we would have dreamed five or six years ago."

While player improvement may be moving along rapidly, as Myers indicates, fan approval, until recently, has been slow. The chase for dollars has hampered the development of the sport in the U.S. somewhat since, in their desire to produce a winner and some revenue, many owners have hired foreign players to lead their teams. Unfortunately, importing players is one of the reasons soccer got off on the wrong foot (so to speak) in the U.S., and the professional teams have been slowly but surely recovering since. And while the American players may be improving, they lost several years of valuable playing and practice time, making their chances of bringing home a World Cup title in 1978 one of the longest shots in history. Still, it will be a spectacle worth watching; the World Cup always is.

3. The Dark Ages in Yankeeland (1900-1968)

America's treatment of soccer in the past was similar to America's initial treatment of any foreigner trying to settle here — the game was tolerated but not widely accepted. Curiously, though its basic concepts were undoubtedly transported across the Atlantic with the *Mayflower,* soccer is considered a newcomer to American sports. Confined to the inner city or small pockets of towns and played by people who spoke broken English, the sport never acquired those nebulous qualities that stamp something as officially American. Soccer groped for real identity in the UmSm, but instead continually came up with a foreign label.

Soccer doesn't have the same homey frontier beginnings as basketball and baseball — two sports considered truly American. Baseball, discovered in 1839 in Cooperstown N.Y., spread from that small town to many others and worked its way *into* the major cities. The roots of baseball were already established in those little country towns around the cities, so when money flowed in to establish teams in the urban areas, there was identification with the sport throughout the country. Because of the land needed to play baseball, spacious rural areas adapted well to the game. While baseball became prominent through the cities where teams located, it had already gained acceptance in the "heartland" — the rural areas of the U.S.A.

Basketball, which, by the way, was discovered by *Canadian*-born James Naismith in Springfield, Mass. in 1891, followed the same kind of rural-to-urban progession as baseball. Although today it is considered a city game, basketball was big in farm country from the start. A simple game to set up, basketball just required a ball and an old peach basket nailed to the barn and anyone could start popping in shots. Of course, basketball caught on quickly in the cities too, for basically the same reasons; but again, by the time the franchises began to grow in the cities, the game's identity had been well established in rural areas as well.

What's so important about acceptance of a sport outside the urban centers? *Because that's what makes it American.* Acceptance comes from there first, the places where they've been "American" for a century or two, not a decade or two. True, it's the city which provides the thrust for widespread recognition; but widespread acceptance comes from the armchairs, kitchens, televisions and farms outside the urban centers.

Baseball, basketball and American football all have earned their acceptance by successfully appealing to the heartland. The tobacco-chewing farm boy who kills squirrels with thrown rocks is discovered by a major league scout, and presto! there's a folk hero for baseball. Basketball catches on in Iowa City, Iowa, where the first intercollegiate game with five on a side was played, and legends begin to channel through the farms to the towns and into the cities where the sport gains widespread popularity. A miner's kid whips everyone in town in arm wrestling, footracing and general brawling, so he winds up wearing a helmet and becoming an American football hero after he draws attention with a city club. Acceptance begins "out there" — in America, where people have time to sit around and swap stories in English about people they knew or saw or played with. That's where an athlete becomes an American in an American sport, even if his name is DiMaggio or Nagurski or even if he's black. To be sure, the ethnic crowds in the city claim them as theirs, but they were nowhere without "out there."

Soccer hasn't been totally accepted yet by "out there" mainly because, as a foreigner, for years it was shoved into the small sections of cities and towns where English was the foreign language and home was across an ocean. It's been in the country longer than any major sport, but accepted? Not yet.

After all, it took years for the various ethnic groups to break out of the cities and successfully integrate America's non-urban society. They had to work, establish themselves, and prove to Americans that they were Americans too. That's where soccer is today in the U.S. — trying to prove it belongs. "Down with xenophobia in the heartlands!" is soccer's cry. And this "furriner" has some American roots for durn sure.

s While soccer did not flourish in ye olde colonial villages, despite the British influence, it was played, but not with the outward passion displayed in Mother England. Not surprisingly, work ethic advocates considered the game a devilish distraction from the austere life they were bound to, and consequently soccer playing was discouraged.

As the U.S. loosened up the game became more acceptable and played more openly, particularly in the

49

76-4460
CENTRAL ARKANSAS LIBRARY SYSTEM
BOOKMOBILE DEPARTMENT
7 J LOUISIANA
I ITLE ROCK, ARKANSAS

New England states and at Ivy League schools. A form of soccer called Ballown was played at Princeton University in 1820, and in 1869 Rutgers and Princeton played the first official varsity soccer game.

Soccer was very nearly officially established as an intercollegiate sport in 1873 when Rutgers and Princeton joined Yale and Columbia in adopting the English rules of soccer as a uniform code for teams to abide by. However, the game was hurt by the Great Harvard Snub. Harvard, leader of leaders among universities, opted for the more physical, non-purist form of soccer called rugby and persuaded other schools to follow the rugby rules. Soccer fans should consider this point before applying to Harvard.

By the late 1800s and the early part of the twentieth century, immigrants were outwardly carrying their enthusiasm for soccer with them. Being the one sport virtually all foreigners had played in their homelands, ethnic soccer groups popped up in major northern cities and not so major ones too, like Fall River, Pawtucket and New Bedford. The games were played with characteristic ethnic pride and toughness. The asphalt playgrounds of Boston or New York were often the soccer "fields", and the contests frequently became mini-wars between Germans and Irish, Italians and Poles, or any assorted mixture of people.

By 1905 the game was becoming more organized on the college level. Harvard, trying to make up for its renegade action in 1873, joined the first Intercollegiate Soccer Association League along with Columbia, Cornell, Haverford and Penn. In 1913, the United States Football Association (now called the United States Soccer Federation, abbreviated USSF) was formed,

50

giving the U.S. a link with the rest of the world through FIFA. In 1914, the Brooklyn Field Club defeated Brooklyn Celtic, 2-1, to win the first U.S. Challenge Cup. Open to all comers at that time, this Cup is still battled for annually by highly ethnic amateur and semi-pro soccer clubs all over the country. The Amateur Cup competition was instituted ten years later, solely for amateur teams, making the game still more public, though the attraction was still highly ethnic.

Van Cortlandt Park in the Bronx was one favorite meeting ground for soccer-playing immigrants in the early 1900s. City kids, bilingual out of necessity, ignored the weekend stickball games and headed for the makeshift soccer fields. Eric Charleson was one of those kids.

Charleson was born in Scotland and came to America at age 15 in 1925. When just a child in Scotland, he remembers kicking a small rubber ball against a wall, as did most other boys, to gain the control necessary for dribbling a soccer ball. When he moved to New York, he continued the practice and before long he was involved in the pick-up games.

"The games were tough then," says Charleson, whose recollections come quickly and vividly. "They were more wide-open games. Today it's all defense; players wander all over with different set-ups. When we played, the center half and outside forwards were the whole ball team. They could swing the ball all around and get the game moving. Plus, most of the kids had seen Europeans play, so they were familiar with that style of play.

"We'd get out on the playground and have 15 to 16 fellas to a side. Teams needed two guys in the goal because guys just bombarded them with shots. A lot of players wore some kind of shin protection for when the kicking

51

got wild. Yep, there were a few scrapes and scratches and black eyes."

Charleson played semi-pro games in the New York area, and watched and played in small but enthusiastic New England towns. "Canadians would come down and play in those New England games and they could play some good ball," says Charleson. "But there was a team out of Bethlehem, Pa., that was great. It was made up of guys who worked in the steel mills. They'd only draw a couple hundred spectators at their home games, but they'd draw 20-30,000 at times on the road."

Bethlehem Steel was just one of many company-sponsored teams of that era. Fielding a team made sense for a company. Not only did it help keep foreign employees happy, and help stave off unions, it was good publicity to have the team playing before a few thousand people. And if they won, so much the better. A few of the other companies that found it expedient to field soccer teams, which were highly regarded, were Robbins Dry Dock, Todd Shipyards, Indiana Flooring Co., Morse Dry Dock and Fleisher Yarn. You may wish to patronize any of these organizations that are still in existence.

Pete Renzulli was another product of New York City park pick-up games. Generally considered the first American-born player to make good in soccer, Renzulli, a goalkeeper, played at McCombs Dam Park in the Bronx, and is a charter member of soccer's hall of fame.

"Renzulli had gone to the park to play baseball — he was a shortstop good enough for semi-pro at 16 — when he saw some guys kicking a soccer ball around," says Charleson. "He was wearing baseball shoes and the guys told him not to kick the ball with those cleats. They told him to get in the goal and try to stop their shots. He stopped every shot they tried."

As a result, Renzulli wound up on their team, St. George, in the New York State Football Association in 1910. He was the only American-born player in the league. He played for several other teams in his career, including Interboro Rapid Transit, New York Protective Association and the New York Giants, who were owned by Charles Stoneham, also owner of the baseball Giants. Renzulli, predictably, was a favorite of New York's Italian community and an energetic teacher; but the Yankees' Tony Lazzeri, whose heyday and background coincided with Renzulli's, is much more widely known even today.

In the twenties, unfortunately for soccer, baseball was the rage and American football was the upcoming game. Soccer was still the game for foreigners.

Though the big publicity chances weren't there, ethnic groups in little New England manufacturing towns and Pennsylvania mining centers played soccer seriously. Where there was industry, there were immigrants and that meant first-generation American families ready to play and watch their national pastime. American Woolen, Shawsheen Mills, Farr Alpaca, Whittal Carpet, and J. P. Coats Thread all had teams, and some of them produced players whose performances, by baseball standards, warranted endorsements and banner headlines. Instead, they received a few extra bucks and a pat on the back at the plant.

Billy Gonsalves' parents were Portugese and they moved to Fall River, Mass., to work in the mills there. Many residents of the milltown were foreign, so Gonsalves, born in Fall River in 1908, grew up playing their game. By the time he was 16, he was playing for Boston in the American Soccer League.

"Gonsalves was the Babe Ruth of American soccer,"

says Charleson, "because he was always scoring goals."

Gonsalves played the typical American soccer circuit, going from town to town, changing teams every few years, but always scoring goals and winning championships.

"Gonsalves played for six National Cup champions in a row (1929-1935) and eight altogether (1942-44)," says Charleson. "He also played on the 1930 and 1934 World Cup teams and was offered a $10,000 salary to play for Botafogo of Brazil around 1935."

Gonsalves had a sometime teammate named Buff Donelli from the coal mines of Morgan, Pa., who performed a soccer feat Pelé never equalled, but made his national fame in American football. From the time he was 15 in 1922 to the time he quit playing amateur soccer in 1929, Donelli led the Senior League of Western Pensylvania in scoring.

"In 1934 Donelli played for the U.S. national team in the World Cup," says Charleson. "The first game was against Mexico, and the U.S. won 4-2. Donelli scored all four of the U.S. goals."

Forget it, Pelé fans, you won't find that one in your man's records.

Donelli was not content to be a roving soccer player, however. He was busily attending school while playing soccer, and in 1930 he graduated from Duquesne University, where he had played football American style. He went on for his M.B.A. at Duquesne and coached freshman football there in 1931.

From 1939-1942 Donelli coached Duquesne's varsity, doubling as head coach of the NFL's Pittsburgh Steelers in 1941. In 1943 he was the line coach for the Brooklyn Dodgers of the NFL when he was persuaded to play for the Morgan Strassers soccer team against the Brooklyn Hispanos as a final performance in soccer. "The Strassers lost that game, 4-1," recalls Charleson, "but Donelli scored their only goal."

Donelli stuck with American football, where there was more recognition and money, and coached Columbia University from 1957-67, winning an Ivy League title in 1961.

The area around Philadelphia's textile mills was also a soccer haven, and Walter Bahr's kicking grounds. Bahr scrambled from game to game as a kid, and played for one of the contry's most famous boys' soccer organizations, Lighthouse Boys Club.

"The game was so popular in that area that Lighthouse had organized leagues for boys from eight years old on up," Bahr says. "And we played a long season, August through the spring. As a 12 year old kid I played about 40 games in a season."

Plus whatever pick-up games he could find. Bahr is proof that even native Americans have the feet to succeed at international soccer if they're taught enough and play enough. He's the guy who assisted in the historic goal which defeated England in 1950 World Cup play.

The game has been in the U.S.A. for a while. Its early-day heroes are localized, not nationalized. The professional American Soccer League, since its inception in 1923 primarily a New England-based league, has appealed to those little soccer hotbeds of the north. The ASL commanded little attention outside New England, though New York provided the local club with television coverage of home games in the fifties. Ethnic leagues like the German-American Soccer League and regional and state semi-pro leagues have sponsored competition for decades. But ethnic is not the same as American and semi-pro doesn't rate nationally. So soccer enthusiasts played their games, went back to their people in their section of town, and remained unknown to the rest of the nation.

Though the sport had some appeal to people who gave it a chance, there have been many who have misunderstood it. Knute Rockne, Notre Dame's most legendary of all its legendary football coaches, liked the game for its demanding physical nature, and saw it as a means of breaking the monotony of regular practice while keeping his players in condition. So one day Rockne stopped practice and lined up his beef in two lines facing each other.

"Men," he said in his best Rockne voice, "today we're going to play a new game. I'm going to put a couple of balls — not footballs — in the middle for you to go after, but you can't touch them with your hands. You're either to kick them — or each other."

Rockne's men, being true Rockne's men, liked the sound of the game. But the team trainer was empty-handed when Rockne turned to get the soccer balls from him, so Rockne sent the trainer looking for them.

Meanwhile, the Notre Dame players were growing impatient, until one finally said, "Aw, the hell with the balls, coach. Let's play the game without 'em!"

Misunderstood. Neglected. A second class citizen. That was soccer U.S.A. for a couple hundred years. Then in 1967, millions of things that Americans love caused America to become interested in the sport.

Bucks. That's what did it. Thoughts of millions of green bucks were generated by the 1966 World Cup games in England and before you can say, "Pelé", three new professional American soccer leagues were formed.

Film clips of the games had been watched enthusiastically by millions of Americans, all the more startling considering that the U.S. team had been eliminated light years before. Plus, there was the little fact that the England vs. West Germany final had grossed £204,805 at the gate, which translated into $573,454. In all, the 32 World Cup matches in England in 1966 grossed $7 million and 1½ million people. The American news media gave the games generous publicity, causing visions of dollar signs to dance in the heads of such moneymen as Lamar Hunt, Jack Kent Cooke, William Clay Ford, William Randolph Hearst II, Jerold Hoffberger and Earl Foreman. The action-packed World Cup games had scarcely faded from the picture tube when these men, not necessarily working together, and a few other monied heavyweights, popped up supporting franchises in one or other of two new leagues - the United Soccer Association (cleverly abbreviated USA - rhetoric for the heartland, no doubt), or the National Professional Soccer League (before it even had a name, the third new league merged with the NPSL). Rival leagues, common goal: bring big-time professional soccer to the U.S. and make some money doing it.

The plan of the men behind the new leagues seemed logical enough. They would simply buy the world's best players and/or teams and bring them to the U.S. to play. Through advertising and media coverage, the plan went, the flames of enthusiasm begun by the World Cup games would make them all rich and soccer would become the rage in American sports.

The two competing leagues (the ASL wasn't even a serious competitor because of its inability to match money with the newcomers) took somewhat different

57

approaches from the start. Representatives of the USA travelled to Europe, Africa, South America and points uncertain, waving lucrative contracts at whole teams. Promises of wealth and fame in the U.S. proved difficult for foreigners to turn down.

Earl Foreman, owner of the Washington soccer franchise of the USA, as well as a part owner of the Philadelphia Eagles and the Baltimore (now Washington) Bullets, acquired his team in typical fashion. He simply signed the entire Aberdeen Dons team of Scotland, brought it to Washington, and changed its name to the Whips after a citywide name-the-team contest.

Using similar persuasive techniques, the USA soon had teams in twelve cities, all totally foreign. The cities and their representative teams were:

Boston (Shamrock Rovers of Ireland)
Chicago (Caligari of Italy)
Cleveland (Stoke City of England)
Dallas (Dundee United of Scotland)
Detroit (Glentoran of Ireland)
Houston (Bangu of Brazil)
Los Angeles (Wolverhampton of England)
New York (Cerro of Uruguay)
San Francisco (ADO of Holland)
Toronto (Hibernian of Scotland)
Vancouver (Sunderland of England)
Washington (Aberdeen of Scotland)

For $25,000 per club and a cut of any television or radio revenue, the USSF sanctioned the USA, giving it official recognition by FIFA and the world as *the* professional league in the States, though all its teams were, in effect, on a soccer-playing vacation there. When their season was finished in America they would all return home, a few thousand dollars apiece richer, in time for their regular season.

The NPSL took a slightly different route, signing local products as well as foreigners. Interestingly enough, the USA overall actually had the higher caliber players, but it was the NPSL which wound up with a $10 million, 10-year television contract from CBS. The NPSL did not want to share its television revenue with anyone, so it was not sanctioned by the USSF and became known as the outlaw league. The outlaw franchises were:

Atlanta	Oakland
Baltimore	Philadelphia
Chicago	Pittsburgh
Los Angeles	St. Louis
New York	Toronto

In general, media coverage of the leagues' escapades prior to their opening days was good. The big-money names, the television contract, the importing of hordes of foreign players, and the whole idea of elevating this foreign game overnight to truly professional status in America, had a certain adventurous air about it. The media in soccer-franchised cities came out with explanations of the games, assorted features and straight coverage. In many cities, to excite fans about the upcoming soccer season, touring world-class foreign teams were brought in to play exhibitions, and they frequently drew well. In Washington, three weeks before the Whips' opener, Eintracht of Germany played Cruzeiro of Brazil in a downpour, but 20,000 fans showed up. As opening day approached, club owners, coaches and players all had reason to be optimistic.

Never have so many smiles turned so quickly to frowns.

Sportswriter Ken Denlinger of the *Washington Post,* who covered the Whips in 1967, recalls their opening day:

"The elements were perfect leading up to the game. Great news coverage, good weather, the momentum of the World Cup games, a good team. But they only drew around 10,000 and, that's when I knew things were going to be tough for them."

Decision makers in the media soured and soon it became tough for the league games to get more than page four or so. In effect, soccer was being told by the media to show it could draw some people if it wanted more coverage.

One month into the season, the NPSL was averaging 5,100 spectators per game, while the USA was averaging 8,850. Since the big-time owners had been used to paying big-time salaries, they originally had felt the $8,000-$12,000 salary range they were paying was a bargain. But not with those attendance figures. The USA teams, with their foreign players playing reasonably good soccer, were still only drawing about half of what they needed to break even. The NPSL, with its mixture of foreign and domestic "talent", was not playing as good a brand of soccer, and in the long run it may be considered somewhat fortunate that not that many people saw NPSL competition.

At the time, of course, the poor attendance was crushing and so were the rumors from CBS — the 10-year contract had a clause in it which said CBS could bail out at any time. The network, discovering its viewership to be a few hundred people or so in assorted cities who could not understand why commercial spots were allowed to interfere with soccer's allegedly continuous action, was looking gratefully at that clause by the middle of the 1967 season.

Little things the owners hadn't counted on were also affecting their teams. Homesick players. Players who couldn't operate stamp and soda machines. Players who brought their whole families to the U.S., expecting the club to pay for housing. Players with names that looked and sounded like unscrambled anagrams. Clubs, like Philadelphia, that had players from so many different countries that a fulltime interpreter had to be kept on the club payroll.

There were big problems too. It's been said somewhere by someone (probably by a New Yorker in New York) that you can't succeed in sports without a thriving franchise in New York. Two early games in 1967 showed the New York Generals, the NPSL's team, to be less than thriving — they drew 2,351 against Baltimore and 3,027 against California. The USA's New York Skyliners club was faring substantially better with a 12,500 average after three games, tops in the league; but there was no television coverage of USA games to show the rest of the country the Big Apple's modestly good soccer and modestly good soccer crowds.

By the end of big-time soccer's first season in the U.S., it was obvious that it had been a big-time disaster. Red ink sales soared in pro soccer cities as teams recorded losses in the vicinity of $400,000 plus per club. So the owners who were game enough to try again in 1968 decided that the first step must be a merger, eliminating intra-city competition in addition to those teams eliminated by financial attrition. The new league was named the North American Soccer League, and the "steamlined" operation of 1968 looked like this:

Atlantic Division	Lakes Division	Gulf Division	Pacific Division
Atlanta	Cleveland	Kansas City	San Diego
Washington	Chicago	Houston	Oakland
New York	Toronto	St. Louis	Los Angeles
Baltimore	Detroit	Dallas	Vancouver
Boston			

The merger made sense, of course, but it was too late. The television contract was lost. The USA clubs incorporated into the NASL could not afford another year of importing entire teams, so they went to a combination of talent, most of it lesser quality players from abroad. In general, the level of play was somewhere between the NPSL's and USA's level of 1967. The media cooled to soccer even more since the sport had failed to prove itself of major league caliber and the American public was still bothered by the foreign identity of this failing sport.

What should have been the lessons of 1967 were not learned well by the teams of 1968. With the old American philosophy that it takes money to make money leading them astray, some of America's wealthiest and allegedly brightest moneymen made some very unwise decisions. They were locked into leases for huge stadiums in which "crowds" were outnumbered by the work crew. The Rose Bowl, with a capacity of 100,423, and Cleveland Stadium, capacity 78,000, are not custom built for trying to revive a sport. Even a good soccer crowd of 10-15,000 looked lost; a realistic gathering of 4,000 looked like so much dust blowing around the empty seats. Renting such places ran into money. In Washington, the Whips leased D.C. Stadium (now Robert F. Kennedy Memorial Stadium), with only a 46,000 seat capacity, for $109,000 per season, covering just 16 home dates.

Then there were the overseas recruiting jaunts of the clubs. General managers again combed the world for players and coaches, sometimes offering amounts far out of line with the club's potential earnings. The St. Louis Stars, for example, on their way to losing a whopping two-year total of $1.5 million by the end of 1968, still paid coach Rudi Gutendorf a fat $50,000 in 1968. On the average, clubs paid management personnel in the $20,000-$30,000 range.

Then there was the whole problem of fan association which was again ignored in 1968. Who did the fans know on the teams? Was there anyone from the suburban U.S. communities, or the campuses, or maybe a big Iowa country boy who could kick that funny looking ball into the net? If we invite someone from the team to speak at a soccer clinic, will he speak English?

1968 was not a very good year. But the haphazard nature of the NASL's operation provided some incidents which today border on slapstick.

In Washington, where the Whips were on their way to losing a two-season grand total of around $600,000, general manager Jerry Cooper went on a worldwide talent hunt, as did most of his colleagues throughout the NASL. Cooper collected players from enough countries to form a miniature U.N.: seven players from Denmark, two from Africa (supposedly the country's top two), two from South America, one from Scotland, one from Spain, and a Hungarian coach. That was the *Washington* Whips.

Whips owner Earl Foreman's international show-case of players had the same drawing problems as most of the rest of the league, and at the end of the 1968 season, Foreman called his team together to tell them they were disbanding. Marc Kammarman, formerly the Whips' traveling secretary, recalls the scene:

"Foreman gathered everyone around and explained that there was no more money. But most of the players didn't speak English so he went through it a couple of times. Pretty soon they started to understand. Finally, Foreman reached into his pocket to show it was empty and then everyone began to catch on.

"One of the South Americans jumped up and said in broken English, 'But Meester Foreman, I have a wife and children. How will I feed them? I will have to go out on a street corner and beg for money.'

"Foreman looked at the player and said, 'Well, if you find a good corner, let me know.'"

Despite the financial difficulties facing the teams, lighter moments were frequently provided by the frequently flamboyant natures of the foreign players. Kammarman, who now is a box lacrosse pusher, worked for $75.00 per week and was road companion, confidant, referee and interpreter for the team. ("I worked my ass off," he claims). Between frequent bursts of laughter, Kammarman recollects the Whips' shenannigans.

"We had a player named Victorio Casa from Argentina who might have been the only one-armed soccer player in the world. The stump he had left was unbelievably strong — guys could chin themselves on it.

"Anyway, Casa was a real lover. We were at the Sheraton in Chicago when I got an early a.m. phone call.

It was the desk clerk and he told me one of the players was down in the lobby harrassing every woman he saw. I asked how he knew it was one of my players and he said, 'There aren't too many other one-armed, Spanish-speaking men with a goatee and moustache in the hotel tonight.' I told him I'd be right down.

"Sure enough, there was Victorio about to put his one arm around a young lady. He was saying, 'Me llamo Victorio . . . Me llamo Victorio.' I broke in and finally persuaded him to go to bed — alone."

Apparently Victorio often followed his stomach with as much enthusiasm as he followed his heart. "We were toward the end of an airplane flight when Victorio got hungry," Kammarman remembers, "and he was sort of sitting in his seat moaning softly, 'ooh, ooh.' A stewardess walked by and asked him if there was a problem. 'Hambre . . . hambre . . . Hungry,' Casa said pointing to his stomach.

"The stewardess explained that there were no more meals scheduled for the flight since we had almost reached our destination. With that, Victorio jumps up and begins biting his good arm and someone yells out to the stewardess in broken English, 'Watch eet, Mees, that's how he lost hees other arm — he ate it!'"

Victorio was sent to the Whips through an agent, as Kammarman remembers it, and prior to a game in Oakland, Victorio's agent called the Whips. "The guy said he had another player for us," says Kammarman. "We told him to send the player down and we'd take a look at him. The guy arrived a day or so before we left for Oakland, so we took him out there with us. He got into the game with a few minutes left, and it wasn't long before we all realized that the guy was worse than bad. He was a complete imposter! It turned out he had relatives he wanted to visit in Oakland."

Then there were the times when Kammarman's best made plans went awry — make that, completely fell apart. "We used to stay at strictly first class places on the road, and I tried to keep everything as smooth as possible," Kammarman says with a ring of true sincerity. "I used to order all the meals in advance so we could just go into the restaurant, sit down, and eat. This way there was no hassle with menus and interpreting orders in eight different languages.

"One morning in Toronto, I was heading toward the restaurant for breakfast when I heard this big commotion inside. I got there and the place was in absolute turmoil. Everyone was waving menus and talking in foreign languages at the same time.

"A hostess ran up to me and asked, 'Are you affiliated with these men?' I had to admit that I was. The team meal I had ordered wasn't available, she explained, so she had told the men to order on their own. This commotion was the result.

"We had started to get things calmed down when who else but Victorio Casa started hunching over and walking around the dining room going, 'Pluck, pluck, pluck, pluck. . . .' His waitress asked me if I knew what he wanted.

"'Easy,' I said. 'He wants two eggs over light.'"

Every hotel, regardless of status, was fair game for the antics of the Whips. At Houston's Shamrock Hotel, Kammarman was presented with a team bill for $1,350 as he checked out. The hotel management would not accept his signing the club's name to the bill, saying they wanted cash only. Kammarman said he'd be right back, headed upstairs and herded the team out the rear of the hotel. He hasn't been back since, and neither have the Whips.

Typical of the personnel problems facing many clubs in '67 and '68 was the volatile mixture of nationalities. According to Kammarman, Washington was no exception, particularly since the coach was a demanding Hungarian named Andre Nagy, a world class player in the fifties. Nagy's major problems stemmed from his inability to communicate with the South American players since they spoke little or no English and no Hungarian at all. This apparently frustrated Nagy so he became even more demanding and quick-tempered as time went by. The result was often a fiery confrontation between Nagy and one or more of his players.

"Everyone hated Nagy," says Kammarman. "He never asked for things; he just told people what to do and people didn't always appreciate that much.

"At our very first away game, in Kansas City, I was in the hotel lobby when I heard my name over the P.A. I went to the desk and there was Roberto Mauro squared off opposite Nagy. I broke it up, but Nagy was so mad he had me book Mauro the first available flight home."

Mauro himself had a little surprise for Nagy and the rest of the Whips. Midway through the season he packed up and left them. The reason? He was returning to Brazil to run for office. Seems he was a city councilman with high aspirations at home.

Obviously, Nagy had his problems and the Whips' beleaguered front office couldn't afford to be sympathetic. Nagy feuded with many people, including one of the Whips' directors, Peter Haley, who at one point suspended the coach prior to a game, leaving public relations director Charley Brotman and the team dentist as coaches. "Brotman set up pennies to try to show the players strategy, but it just didn't work all that well," Ken Denlinger recalls with a chuckle.

Eventually, the frustrated Nagy was fired by Haley after a clash over player personnel. "Nagy was so mad," Denlinger says, "that the worst thing he could think of to say was, 'Mr. Haley's knowledge of soccer does not come up to my ankle.'"

Throughout the NASL in 1968 the teams pulled out all the public relations gimmicks imaginable to boost attendance. There were giveaways, discount tickets, special nights, booster clubs and the like from coast to coast. Still, the league's per-game average attendance was only 3,400; 20,000 was considered break-even.

Charley Brotman, the Whips' public relations director, is no newcomer to sports promotion, but he didn't have much luck in the early days of pro soccer in the U.S. Prior to the Whips opener in 1968 he promoted a benefit game for Children's Hospital involving Santos of Brazil and its star Pelé. He took out a rain insurance policy which said it must rain ⅜ of an inch or more to collect. "It rained enough to keep people away, but not enough to collect," he laments. For the Whips, Brotman dug deep into the recesses of his clever mind for a device that would attract fans.

"I really feel I did everything possible," he says looking back. "I believe you can make a person go someplace he never thought he'd go, but you have to have the right conditions and inducements. So I zeroed in on the birthday box idea. If a kid came to a game on his birthday, he'd get a ball, presented by a player, have his name put on the scoreboard's Magic Message, and he'd get a bunch of other little items too.

"We had family days with special prices if the whole family came to the game. We had drawings of numbers that corresponded to numbers in the programs for prizes. We even had a contest where if you kicked the ball into the goal with no one guarding it, you could keep the ball."

At various points during the season, Brotman either tried, or thought about trying, things such as Whipettes (female cheerleader types) walking around the stadium saying, "Cigars, cigarettes, Whips tickets?", instituting a babysitting service during games, and giving away multi-colored soccer socks.

Brotman's retrospective analysis of the Whips' failure applies to the whole league for 1967-68:

"There was a lack of association with the sport. The game frustrated fans because they weren't used to it; people hadn't experienced the game enough. People had seen the big buildup since 1966 and when they came out to the games, they were disappointed in the results. They didn't know a corner kick from a goal kick. What's worse, there was no personal identity with the players.

"Foreign spectators were supposed to provide the nucleus of fans in a lot of cities until the Americans caught on. Well, in Washington we figured embassy row would flock to the games. Instead, some of the kitchen help came, but the upper classes held out for free tickets."

And hundreds of thousands of others held out around the country too. Losses swelled to over a million dollars for some clubs, and "out of business" signs popped up in soccer team offices throughout the country. Soccer was swirling down the drain, and after the 1968 season only a ring was left around the tub, a ring composed of teams in just five cities — Dallas, Atlanta, Kansas City, St. Louis and Baltimore. That's all that was left to try again. Soccer in the U.S. had gone from a mountain to a molehill financially in just two short years. In those two years the game had done little to endear itself to the heartland. It was still a game played for foreigners by foreigners, plus, it was a money-loser. People still weren't sitting around taverns, living rooms and kitchens swapping stories about pro soccer stars.

It looked as though a prophecy made by Washington's Hungarian coach, Andre Nagy, would never come to pass in Washington or anywhere else. Nagy, speaking to Ken Denlinger about soccer's future in the U.S. and Washington, stood outside D.C. Stadium and said, "Someday, this place will be full for soccer!"

4.   Renaissance (1969-1974)

20/20 Hindsight Department:

"In the early years we forgot to educate the people" — Ted Howard, Director of Administration, NASL, February, 1975.

"In '67 and '68 American soccer club owners and the American people were conned. Clubs felt they had an unlimited supply of money and they spent a lot of it; they got some good players, but not the world's best." — Dennis Viollet, Washington Diplomats head coach and former player, April, 1975.

"The original leagues had an agreement to keep salaries down, but a couple of players got $20-30,000, and pretty soon salaries were not in line with income." — Walter Bahr, soccer coach, Penn. St., June, 1975.

"The biggest problem in 1967 was the formation of two leagues, because it forced people into greater expenditures than necessary at that time. Had they combined their forces and gone into a development program for a year or two to prepare for the pro level while developing the youth level, the sport would have arrived by now." — Phil Woosnam, former General

Manager of the Atlanta Chiefs, and currently Commissioner of the NASL February, 1975.

Some men will take on anything.

The offices are not large and they're definitely not jockish. There are no action photographs adorning the walls, which strikes some sort of ironic note to the visitor since the NASL's headquarters are located several stories above the Kodak exhibit in New York. There are sports magazines scattered around the waiting room, but, again ironically, only one magazine other than *Soccer Monthly* has a soccer-related story in it. The offices seem to reflect the league in February, 1975 — low key but very busy, with the potential to attract attention. Three secretaries all seem genuinely hard at work, and one shows that attention-getting potential at the expense of a stray Fuller brush man who wanders in pedalling his wares. The secretary stops typing and interrupts his pitch in vintage New Yorkese, "I want a Fuller brush right now like I want a giraffe right now."

Had it been 1969, the Fuller brush man would no doubt have been invited into the NASL offices by the commissioner himself, been offered some coffee (instant, it's cheaper), and received a batch of tickets to hand out to his best customers. He might have even sold a brush, a good stiff one, since the commissioner sported a very jockish flattop.

Phil Woosnam was commissioner then, as he is now, but a lot of things are different now including the hair (which has evolved to executive length and styling), the .offices,. and the state of soccer in the U.S.A.

"When I took over as commissioner of the NASL in January of '69, I asked Clive Toye (a former soccer writer for the *London Daily Express* and one of the moving forces behind soccer in America, currently the general manager of the New York Cosmos) to come to Atlanta with me," Woosnam recalls. "We started in the basement of Atlanta Stadium in the same dressing room we had used after winning the championship a few months earlier (when Woosnam was general manager of the Atlanta Chiefs).

"Toye and I were the total administrative staff. We put some desks up and got to work." With a straight face Woosnam adds, "I was in the right place at the right time."

This was not Woosnam's subtle Welsh humor surfacing. He felt fortunate even then, with what was perhaps the smallest and most financially insecure league in professional sports history. But Woosnam is an optimist with a sound and stable basis. Woosnam has been so secure and confident about the NASL, he could make a normal person fidgety: the unflappable Englishman personified. Didn't he see what was stacked up against him? Wasn't he aware of soccer's alien status in the U.S.? Didn't Woosnam know that soccer's credibility in financial and media circles was practically nil?

Balderdash! He knew: just pour a cup of tea, relax and listen.

"The feeling in 1968 and 1969 was that the new American breed could not work out the problems soccer faced," Woosnam admits. "People refused to believe that we all could get together. We lost those leaders from '67 and '68, unfortunately, and it gave the sport an image it hadn't had previously. We had to overcome all those prejudices. Although the merger took place, I never really

73

felt it cleared up the situation. I never felt there was real unity among all the clubs during 1968.

"Unfortunately there was too much brainpower, effort, time and expense put into lawsuits that developed out of the league's differences of opinions. They set their sights too high and became frustrated because of the legal actions.

"The major reason we stayed alive was because Lamar Hunt stayed on. We had no credibility except for him. He had a track record in sports."

An old sports tale has it that in the early days of the American Football League, Lamar Hunt's Kansas City Chiefs franchise, like so many other AFL teams, lost a million dollars in one season. An interested sportswriter asked Hunt's father how long Lamar could continue losing that kind of money. "Well," Daddy Hunt supposedly replied, "if he keeps that up, he'd better start worrying in about a hundred and fifty years."

Lamar Hunt is widely credited with salvaging the AFL in its lean years. His World Championship of Tennis is a growing force in that sport. And, after the 1968 NASL season, when American soccer was at the lowest point of its brief history, Hunt held fast to his Dallas franchise and may well have saved the sport from extinction in the U.S., though he plays down his role.

"Phil gives me too much credit," Hunt says. "He's the guy who went out and knocked on doors. I gave a degree of stability at the time because of my involvement in other sports. But Phil was the major stabilizing force."

Hunt rejects as "completely false" the rumor that he financially supported three of the five remaining franchises in 1969. "Dallas is the only soccer team I've ever had a financial interest in. Even after 1968 I felt the idea of pro soccer still had merit in the U.S. I felt it was something that was so big in the rest of the world it just had to catch on. Besides, I'm a sucker for the entertainment industry and that's what sports are. That's why I stayed in, but my financial support only went to the Dallas Tornado.

"Sure, I felt it might all collapse; we were very close to it a number of times. Unfortunately, there were some people around who were interested in just picking the bones."

Even with Hunt's bankroll and Woosnam's optimistic fervor, the five-team league very nearly completed the fall of soccer in America. Woosnam's original plan for 1969 was an attempt at whetting America's interest by bringing in first division teams from around the world to represent each of the five remaining cities for the first half of a 16 game schedule. After spectators were hooked on the game, Woosnam's theory went, less expensive, less talented, but more stationary clubs would take over for the second half of the season.

The season opened in Baltimore with two of England's finest teams competing — Wolverhampton, representing Kansas City, and West Ham United, representing Baltimore. Woosnam's hair stood further on end when the attendance was announced — 5,128 spectators for a game that, in England, would have undoubtedly drawn 50,000. People were not hooked and it became obvious to Woosnam that Americans weren't even familiar with the bait.

Even before the 1969 season began, Woosnam had imposed a $250,000 operating ceiling on teams, a far more reasonable level than the $600 thousand to a million level of '67 and '68. With the flopping of Plan A, Woosnam realized he had to put his considerable energies into Plan B.

"The role of the league office was to establish a base for the league which hadn't existed previously," he says in his carefully paced voice. "The sport had been in the country for years, particularly in northern cities with strong ethnic groups, but there was not a great American interest in the sport.

"The league had to establish a working relationship with every level of the sport — pros, college, high school, youth — so that all forces would work together. I had to get to know the important people. I had to get to know everyone."

Woosnam hit the roads, the airways, and the tracks of America. He talked soccer to anyone willing to listen. Toye and others helped, but Woosnam led the way by example. You have to believe Woosnam could sell cats to dogs. With league attendance hovering on the shy side of 3,000 for 1969, he was out selling the game, establishing those important roots in points distant. Since some of the original clubs had begun some grassroots movements of their own before going under, Woosnam had a small nucleus to work with in some cities. And in cities where none existed, he and the other pioneers began one.

Slowly, they were sweeping away the ruins and removing the tarnish of two years.

By 1970, the NASL was operating out of office space in Atlanta and the league gained two and lost one. It lost the Baltimore franchise and gained Washington and Rochester, N.Y. The fact that Washington, under new management, wanted a franchise although the Whips had failed, was a heartening sign for the NASL, as was the Rochester group's interest in the league. Attendance inched slowly upward.

In 1971, the league expanded to eight teams with Kansas City dropping out and Toronto, Montreal, and New York entering. The new teams bought into the league for a measley $10,000. But an unexpected problem began to develop for the league, a problem that plagues it still to a certain extent today. As the grassroots interest in soccer began to grow and awareness of the sport began to increase, fans began to realize that the soccer they were seeing was of pretty low caliber. There was a growing interest in the sport, but not at the quality level the NASL was offering. The reduced budgets and the restraints in spending imposed by Woosnam's office meant the hiring of many players involved in third and fourth division play in Europe.

"In general, the type of player who comes here from overseas is either a young kid, or a guy who's over the hill, or a malcontent," Walter Bahr claims, expressing a belief he's held for years. "I can see bringing over kids without family ties over there, but not the others."

Then there were the old problems of fan identification with American players and how to promote the teams. In St. Louis, 1969 had been a crucial year. The club felt that being in the same town as perennial collegiate soccer power, St. Louis University, there was no reason to ignore the local talent. The Stars were the first team to become really committed to an Americanization program, and their 1975 team boasted seven American starters. But the early days of Americanization were difficult. From 1969-1971 they won only 14 of 64 games, while Washington, playing without any Americans, won its division in 1970 en route to a combined two-year record of 22 wins, 12 losses, and 14 ties.

With or without American players, teams still only averaged 3,400 fans per game in 1971, but that was the creeping kind of progress Woosnam was conditioned for. Smaller budgets, smaller stadiums and smaller salaries made for smaller losses. So while crowds were no larger than they were in '67 and '68, the lower cost of operation made more tolerable financial losses (if any financial loss can, in fact, be called tolerable). Woosnam's optimism was further fed by the re-entry of a New York franchise in 1971. This time the New York club, named the Cosmos, had strong financial backing in the form of Warner Communications, producer of film stars, cable television, and other forward-moving operations. Warner meant a little security and a lot of credibility.

That promotional angles were drying up was perhaps best illustrated in the Nation's Capital in 1971. The Darts, as the '70-'71 version was named, had everything going against them. No Americans, games played at 4:00 p.m. on Sundays at Catholic University, a school difficult for residents of Maryland, Virginia, and even D.C. to get to, a $1,700 phone bill and a public address announcer who criticized the play-by-play over the P.A. After giving away everything except money to attract customers, the team pulled out the promotional plug and brought in none other than Murray the K to orchestrate a game to rock and roll.

Washington was in Miami by 1972 and Murray the K was still trying to figure out how to make headers and penalty shots fit rhythmically into Rolling Stones music.

The NASL's stabilization period was in its third year by 1972 and the league was being carefully nurtured to health by Woosnam. Little things were beginning to break right as the league streamlined its operation even more. The briefest schedule in NASL's history, 14 games, seemed like an odd direction for a "growing" sport to go, but it was a calculated moneysaver. Woosnam knew the expansion years were just around the corner, and he wanted a stable base for growth. There were encouraging signs for the league, like St. Louis where the Stars doubled their attendance and income over 1971 Dallas drew 24,742 to a 0-0 tie with the Moscow Dynamo, 10-time Russian champs. The quality of play around the league was still at about the 1971 level, but fans began to identify with the teams in their city just a little, and average attendance jumped to 5,200 per game.

Plus, New York seemed to be working out. The league offices were operating there for the second year in a row, having completed the psychological transition of moving from the musty low-rent Atlanta lockerroom to the status of musty high rent New York. More important was the psychological advantage of a successful New York team, at least on the basis of won-loss if not profit-loss. The New York Cosmos won the Northern Division title and then beat the American-laden St. Louis Stars, 2-1, for the league title. The Championship game was played in the rain at Hofstra University Stadium before a modest crowd of 6,102.

The Cosmos also had the NASL's MVP and leading scorer in 1972, a six-two, 195 pound (large for soccer), bearded, Afroed native of Bermuda named Randy Horton. Scoring 22 points on nine goals and four assists, Horton eventually attracted attention by becoming a headmaster — that is, he mastered head shots, regularly banging in goals off his skull, and he also became the fulltime headmaster of a school in Bermuda. Horton would commute from Bermuda to New York, head in a goal or two, and catch the return flight to head up his school.

79

Randy Horton, one of the NASL stars during the renaissance years, and the league's Most Valuable Player in 1972. *Washington Diplomats photo.*

Problems: they were still around even with increasing attendance, the improving New York connections, and the success of St. Louis' largely American product. Foreigners still comprised 85% of the league's players. None of the Americans had national star power. Woosman, in a sales performance Dale Carnegie himself couldn't match, was forced to find new owners for Atlanta, Rochester and Miami (which had been the Washington Darts in '70 and '71) in a little over a month's time.

The Miami move proved disastrous in '72. From the outset the club suffered an ideitity crisis, and it got worse as the season went on. The team began its search for a name with the traditional name-the-team gimmick. Showing a keen unawareness of soccer's struggle to escape the foreign image, club officials chose the name Gatos, Spanish for cats. The Miami Cats would have been a nice, if blatantly hip compromise, but Gatos immediately flashes a foreign image. Of course, there's a large Spanish-speaking population in Miami which management was trying to appeal to, disregarding the Americanization movement.

Had the Gatos played better soccer they might have drawn the ethnic crowd, but they started off badly, drawing a paltry 1,762 to their opening day loss, and went downhill to a 3-3-8 season record. Along the way, three players were fired by general manager Norm Sutherland, and head coach Sal De Rosa quit with over half the season remaining. He was never replaced.

More problems.

National television was out of the question without a coast-to-coast market. The fact that Toronto led the league in average attendance in 1972 with 7,274 fans per game did not speak well for United States based clubs. And Philadelphia, where a new franchise was awarded for the 1973 season, two months before opening day had signed just two players, had no office, and no name.

But 1973 may well go down in U.S. soccer history as The Year of the Turning Point.

To begin with, Miami somehow attracted new owners who also held financial interests in the Miami Dolphins of American football fame. The new owners began by taking a bold step forward and changed the team's name from Gatos, which people thought was a misspelling of the more logical name Gators, to Toros, which people thought was a misspelling of the equally illogical name Tacos.

The owners' next step showed they at least had more knowledge of a soccer team's basic needs than the previous owner had — they hired a coach, and a good one at that. The Toros hired John Young, an assistant coach with the 1972 NASL champion New York Cosmos. Then, by beefing up publicity, the club astounded the league by selling 2,400 season tickets, an NASL record at the time. Later in the season, a crowd of 22,474 attended a no-contest contest between Pelé's Santos team and the Toros, won by Santos 6-1. By the end of '73, Miami had more than doubled its home attendance figures over 1972, averaging over 6,000 including a crowd of 12,766 for its opening game of the season.

In fact, looking at the attendance figures around the league for home openers had to make Phil Woosnam feel like all those nationwide treks had been worthwhile Average attendance for the first home games of the 1973 season was 9,758 compared to 5,861 in 1972. The newly franchised Philadelphia team had acquired a name, the

Atoms, and a lot of fans — 21,700 showed up for the home opener after a parade of 3,000 youngsters in full soccer dress welcomed the team. There were 19,342 fans in rainy Dallas' Texas Stadium, and 9,075 in New York for home openers in those cities. And, of course, Miami pitched in with its surprising turnout.

The nine-team league in 1973 was split into three divisions and the schedule was expanded slightly to 19 games. The three-division, three-team format forced all teams to at least appear to be contenders for a period of time, adding a little more interest to the season. League play also grew more competitive because of the alignment. But most important of all, a couple of genuine American-born stars crashed the sport. One of them, Kyle Rote Jr., was even the son of a household name, although senior's name was made in American football.

When the name Rote first started appearing in soccer stories, some people felt the need to check and make sure it wasn't short for Rotelli or Rotevick. But sure enough, it was Rote, blond hair and as American as an All-American. Finally, an American soccer player who could command national attention. He was worthy, too, racking up 10 goals and 10 assists for 30 points to lead the league in scoring. In one quick season Rote had become the first American to ever lead the league in scoring and the first American to win Rookie of the Year.

Rote tied for the honor of being first American to lead a team to the NASL finals, sharing that with another blondie, goalie Bob Rigby, a local boy making good with that last-minute franchise in Philly. Rigby, also a rookie, set an NASL record for goalkeepers with his .62 goals against average.

The 1973 Philadelphia Atoms, a Gas House Gang

type group, led the league in attendance with a record 11,382 per game average, and entertainment. With an excellent grasp of how to Americanize a soccer team, the Atoms exploded from the start.

Tom McCloskey, Atoms owner, was reluctant about buying the franchise at first. His past experiences in sports ownership justified his scepticism as a main financial backer of the extinct Philadelphia Ramblers · in the Eastern Hockey League; president of the Liberty Bowl football game which fled Philly; and a founder of Cloverlay, the corporation which owned Joe Frazier's contract. And, of course, one soccer team had failed in Philadelphia already — the Spartans of '68. But McCloskey had a friend in Texas, Lamar Hunt — a well-respected soccer pusher — telephoning him and meeting with him at San Francisco's Fairmount Hotel, saying that a McCloskey owned soccer franchise would work in Philadelphia. Hunt has made some pretty good financial decisions in his time, so McCloskey investigated and discovered that 44 colleges were playing soccer in the nearby Delaware Valley, and high school and youth programs were steadily increasing. McCloskey decided to put up the money for the franchise — $25,000, up $15,000 from 1971.

Once into the racket, McCloskey hit the streets to sell his stuff. For a coach he went after Al Miller, a former All-American soccer player at nearby East Stroudsburg State College who was not without color.

When Miller left East Stroudsburg, he jumped right into the golf coach's job at Albright College where he compiled a perfect .00 vinning percentage. Miller then sorted out the deluge of offers and moved on as admissions officer and soccer coach at New Paltz State

84

College in New York, an all girls school in its first year of coed. From there, Miller went to Hartwick College, and if you've heard of Hartwick you either went there, live in upstate New York, or you're a dyed-in-the-wool soccer fan.

At Hartwick, Miller found a school with a soccer team supported by the town, cheerleaders, radio, television, and a band. Miller took the tiny school to a second place national ranking in 1970, and compiled a 64-12-2 record in six years. Then in 1973 he went on to engineer the Philadelphia Atoms story.

The Philadelphia press enjoyed Miller's local color. He told the media what it was like growing up in the Dutch town of Ono, Pa., a town that supposedly got its name at the first town meeting, when everyone kept saying, "Oh no!" to the names being suggested. Stories of Miller attending school where all eight grades were taught in one room, and the discovery that his childhood nickname of Bosh had the highly insignificant Dutch translation of "turnip", gave Miller the element soccer in the U.S.A. needed most — someone with roots.

Miller and McCloskey continued strengthening their American link when it came time to choose players. In an excellent move publicity-wise and soccer-wise, five of their first six signers were Americans who had played their college soccer in, or had some other link with, the Philadelphia area: Charlie Duccilli of Temple University, an All-American who had set the Temple career scoring record with 66 goals; Bob Rigby of East Stroudsburg State; Bob Smith of Rider College; Casey Bahr of Navy, son of Walter; and Stan Startzell, a three-time All-American from the University of Pennsylvania.

McCloskey okayed some good investments for the

team. The winner of the name-the-team contest received an all-expenses paid trip to London for the English Soccer Championships. And McCloskey sent Miller and his still incomplete Atoms squad on a 10-day trip to train in Lilleshall, England in April. Lilleshall is the soccer dream facility: with 11 outdoor fields, one indoor, and a hotel/dormitory complex, it is the site where England's national team works out.

Miller knew Lilleshall would impress the few Atoms he had, especially the Americans. In addition, it gave him the chance to fill out the squad with British players who played the fast-moving type of soccer he prefers. Miller likes his teams in superior physical condition, and Lilleshall meant the chance to train hard in a total soccer environment.

By the time the 1973 season began, Philadelphians were curious about this colorful, largely local soccer bunch, and the more the people saw the more they liked. Americans Rigby and Smith played outstanding defensive soccer all year long, while Britons Andy "The Flea" Provan and Jim Fryatt led the offense.

Provan, a spunky five-five, 140 pound forward, finished third in the league in scoring and was a crowd pleaser with his hustling play. Once, in a game against the Cosmos before 9,168 fans in Philadelphia, New York's six-two, 195 pound Randy Horton leaped into the air and landed on Provan. Incensed, Provan jumped to his feet and began shaking his fist in Horton's face. Looking straight up into Horton's beard, Provan slapped Horton, touching off a scuffle which resulted in both players being ejected, but giving the tiny Provan some giant-sized publicity around town.

The Atoms' success was also due to a classic example

Peter Silvester of the Baltimore Comets shows some of the form that scored 14 goals and won him MVP honors in 1974. *Photo by Steve Hammond.*

Randy Horton. *Photo by Mark Rattner.*

of mutual appreciation. The fans appreciated the Atoms' gutsy, winning soccer, and the players appreciated the fans — and they let them know it by taking every opportunity to talk about how great the crowd support was. The Atoms were more approachable than athletes in other sports, taking turns showing up at Veterans Stadium an hour-and-a-half early to sit at an on-field picnic area and talk informally with groups of fans as part of the team's "meet-the-fan" policy (notice it wasn't a "meet-the-player" policy).

Miller prodded his team to top performance with dramatics when he had to. Once, with the Atoms losing at halftime, the players went to the locker room expecting Miller to raise hell. Instead, he was sitting on a bench reading newspapers. Finally, just before the second half began, Miller looked up, tore the papers into shreds and said, "Here's what I think of your press clippings. If you guys would learn to play soccer as well as you read, maybe you'd be getting the job done out there!" The Atoms went on to win.

On the field the team showed a flair for dramatics of their own. Their defense was so stingy, defensemen Derek Trevis, Roy Evans, Chris Dunleavy, Smith and Rigby became known as the "No Goal Patrol". There was a string of 12 undefeated games from May 6 to July 7, and three goals in three minutes against Rochester, both NASL records. In the final regular season game, with a playoff berth wrapped up, the Atoms hosted the St. Louis Stars, who needed a win to make the playoffs. With no extra reason to be up for the game, the Atoms crushed the Stars 5-1 before 18,375 fans. Provan scored three goals and Philadelphians knew they were in love.

One week later, on August 18, a crowd of 18,766 saw

the Atoms beat Toronto in the semifinals, 3-0, to earn a crack at the NASL championship against Dallas, which had beaten the Cosmos, 1-0, before 9,009 in Texas three days earlier.

Phil Woosnam himself couldn't have written a more perfect setting for the 1973 championship game. The Cinderella Atoms against Hunt's Tornado, one of only three teams (St. Louis and Atlanta being the others) operating since American pro soccer's shakey start in 1967. And the American factor: league leading scorer, American Kyle Rote, against league leading goalie, American Bob Rigby. Rote, who had scored or set up the winning goal in six of Dallas' 11 victories, versus Rigby, who had held six teams scoreless during the season.

Adding to the tension surrounding the game was the announcement, just days prior to the championship game, that key loan players from both teams were being recalled to begin their seasons in Great Britain. Dallas was losing the aggressive Ricky Reynolds, in addition to John Collins and Nick Jennings. But Philadelphia seemed to be getting hurt worse since their popular scoring duo of Andy Provan and Jim Fryatt were being called home.

Philadelphia fans responded emotionally to the announcement as did Fryatt and Provan. Eyes watering, and not from hay fever, the two part-time Atoms boarded a plane for England just five days before the Dallas game, waving goodbye to fans and their stateside teammates. Miller said, "I tried everything. I even told Southport (the British club) that Jim's wife was pregnant and couldn't travel and that Andy had broken his leg after our victory celebration. They didn't go for it."

As a result, Miller's starting lineup included six

Americans, and the results were realistically and symbolically favorable. The Atoms exploded while the Tornado dissolved before a record NASL championship game crowd of 18,824 partisan Texans. Briton Chris Dunleavy of the Atoms, playing a bumping, physical game, held Rote scoreless while Rigby made save after save to thwart Dallas. Philadelphia won, 2-0, to become the first expansion team in any professional sport in the U.S. to ever win a league championship in its first season.

Philadelphians, who had been able to watch the game on local television, turned out not in thousands like they would for football or hockey or basketball, but in hundreds at least to greet the team, which arrived at the airport two hours late.

The Philadelphia Atoms of 1973 were unique among sports' many underdog stories. The Atoms were in fact invisible six months before their championship season began. But once they became visible and started playing their games before some of the largest American pro soccer crowds up to that time, they captured the imagination and emotion of a major city in the United States, a city with established pro teams in football, baseball, basketball and hockey. It was the first time a U.S. soccer team had ever held that kind of attention over a season. The 1973 Atoms gave genuine hope for soccer's survival as a pro sport in the U.S.A.

There were other encouraging signs in 1973, perhaps not of the same magnitude as the Atoms, but encouraging nonetheless. Average attendance throughout the NASL climbed to 6,290. In Dallas, Kyle Rote Jr.'s influence showed at the gate as attendance rose 86% over 1972 with an average crowd of 7,465 per game. In New York, an American star with the charismatic name of Joey Fink was born to Warner Communications, Inc. Fink, a soccer All-American out of N.Y.U. and a Brooklyn native, came in second in Rookie of the Year voting, sandwiched between fellow Americans Rote and Rigby. Another young American, Al Trost of the St. Louis Stars, played well enough to make honorable mention on the 1973 NASL All-Star team.

On the financial side, things were still red. Even the Atoms lost money in 1973. But for most cities, the red was not as bright as it had been in the recent past.

Two clubs, Montreal and Atlanta, did fold after 1973. Montreal, where soccer had difficulty catching on because of Canadian football, National League baseball, and National Hockey League hockey, collapsed after a three-year record of 13-29-14. Montreal's major contribution in three years was to provide the NASL with the weirdest all-time nickname — l'Olympique de Montreal. They could have even used Gatos and come out ahead.

The loss of Atlanta was the most serious smudge on 1973's otherwise semi-clean slate of accomplishments. A pro soccer city since 1967, champions in 1968 and 1971, Atlanta had some soccer tradition. But it didn't have the financial staying power, despite the fact that the 1973 operation was run by Omnigroup, Atlanta's sports biggies who also own basketball's Atlanta Hawks and hockey's Atlanta Flames. In the April 1973 issue of *Pro Soccer Report,* Omnigroup President Bill Putnam was quoted as saying, "we're in this thing to stay. We didn't get in just for a year or two, but for as long as it takes to build up the sport here."

But Atlanta suffered its worst year ever on the field, winning just three games, and had few Americans playing. So the city where the Woosnam era had begun was now out of the game, putting a major damper on a generally bright season.

Within the head of Phil Woosnam, beneath the butch haircut, events of 1973 were soon being channelled into soccer's next step. "The most important factor facing us at that time was to expand the league and cover all of the country," the butch-less Woosnam of '75 recalls. "The expansion to 15 teams in 1974 was a very critical step and we decided to take it in December 1973."

The NASL had become a hot, but still highly speculative, property and cities now had to sell Woosnam after years of the reverse. Woosnam could now announce the "awarding" of franchises, whereas not so long ago he was finding franchises. For $75,000, franchises in 1974 went to old-faces Washington, in for a third shot at pro soccer, and Baltimore, a dropout after the 1969 season. In addition, established sports markets Boston, Denver, and Los Angeles were awarded teams. And, in a move where Woosnam must have consulted his local palmist, the virgin territories of San Jose, Seattle, and Vancouver, B.C. received approval for league play.

Four of the new franchises — Washington, Baltimore, Denver, and Los Angeles — flunked at the turnstiles, averaging in the 3,500-5,500 category (which would have looked good way back in, say, 1971).

The other four newcomers finished in the top six. Both the San Jose Earthquakes and the Seattle Sounders broke the previous NASL total attendance mark of 129,236 set in 1968 by the Kansas City Spurs. In 10 games San Jose averaged 16,576 while Seattle averaged 13,495 in 11 games, including seven consecutive sellouts at the end of the year. The Vancouver Whitecaps, who frequently

92

started ten Canadians, averaged 10,098 and Beantown, an important sports city, averaged 9,642.

Unlike 1973, when only Philadelphia averaged over 8,000 per game, 1974 found Philadelphia (11,784) and Dallas (8,469), in addition to the expansion teams, surpassing the 8,000 mark. For the year, the average NASL per-game attendance in 1974 was 7,825, not quite enough for any club to finish out of the red, but moving in the right direction.

Helping the sport was Kyle Rote Jr.'s victory in the 1974 Superstars competition. There, among all those highly paid household sports names, was a pro soccer player turning back opponent after opponent in event after event. Modest, competitive, and only 23 years old, Rote gave soccer some sorely needed recognition, if not total acceptance, before a large national television audience.

But for all its overall success at the gate, 1974 was a year of growing pains. Plans and operations for various clubs seemed ill-fated or ill-designed. While the Sounders, for example, could probably have filled a larger stadium, Dallas' reasonably good attendance figure paled in spacious Texas Stadium. Only San Jose, with a stadium seating just over 18,000, seemed in the ideal-sized home.

In Rochester, where the ambitious Lancers had 20,000-seat Holleder Memorial Stadium redecorated for the start of the season, attendance fluttered around 5,000 for most of the season, leading to one of history's most illogical promotions. To attract soccer fans, the Lancers invited Gina Lollabrigida to attend a game. She accepted and the club promoted Gina from various angles. The result was roughly the same average-size crowd and a lot of people wondering just what the hell Gina Lollabrigida had to do with soccer in Rochester.

In Washington, the Diplomats took over where the Whips and Darts had left off, when they made news in a thoroughly negative fashion. With a few lost souls wandering around R.F.K. Stadium in Washington for the game against the Philadelphia Atoms on July 9, attendance was announced at 3,325. When a few members of the press choked on their No-Doz at the figure, public relations director Debbie Goldstein agreed that the crowd seemed smaller, and she refused to spout the management line. Minutes later, a member of the Diplomats' brass made Ms. Goldstein the ex-public relations director for her veracity and audacity. As a result of the incident, a club official threatened to revoke the press credentials of Washington *Post* reporter Leonard Shapiro for reporting the incident in the paper, and the club refused to sell copies of the newspaper *Soccer Weekly,* which also carried the story, at Diplomats games. The Diplomats, a team in need of positive press, seemed to be trying their best to make Richard Nixon's press relations look cordial by comparison.

The New York Cosmos switched the site of their 1974 games from Hofstra Stadium in Long Island, where they had played for three years and were beginning to establish some identity, to crumbling Downing Stadium on Randalls Island. A product of the 1930s work project days, rutted, dingy, and lacking hot showers, the stadium was almost as bleak as the Cosmos' 4-14-2 season record. Both the team and the stadium were unattractive and, predictably, New York's average attendance plummetted to 3,600.

Frustration over disappointing attendance (6,700

average) stimulated some potentially harmful ideas in Toronto. Bruce Thomas, owner of the Metros, announced toward the end of June that he would give a dollar to the first thousand kids into the stadium on the condition that they cheer loudly for the home team. Realizing that when you start paying people to cheer for your product you're at the bottom of the proverbial barrel, Woosnam rushed a cable to Toronto and squelched the idea.

Despite improving upon 1973's record-setting attendance figures, the Philadelphia Atoms spent much of the 1974 season skidding. Things started off ominously for Al Miller when Roy Evans, a key member of Philadelphia's "No Goal Patrol", was unable to play because of commitments with England's Liverpool club. There were also a couple of internal problems which centered around mutterings by an American player or two who had indicated, following 1973's championship victory over Dallas, that the Atoms didn't need any Englishmen to win, referring to Andy Provan and Jim Fryatt who had been recalled by their Southport team five days before the Dallas game. Then, as the season progressed, the Atoms became so desperate for a midfielder who could take charge that Miller imported Chris Fagan from England. Though Fagan arrived in Philadelphia just hours before a game after 22 hours of travel, Miller played him.

It was also a year for management-level explosions. In Denver, the newly enfranchised Dynamos weren't a fourth of the way through their season when general manager Norm Sutherland publicly berated the team's slow start. Al Miller press-lashed some of his players, mercifully leaving them anonymous, for lack of hustle.

Los Angeles Aztecs coach Alex Perolli, after taking his expansion team to three consecutive wins at the start of the season, publicly criticized goalie Kevin Barclay's play, and fired him barely 24 hours after a 4-3 victory over St. Louis. And when Dallas coach Ron Newman remarked prior to playing St. Louis that the Stars started too many Americans, the St. Louis players took the field and presented each member of the Tornado a small American flag.

While the quality of play did not improve greatly, the style did, though perhaps not in the purist sense. If less than world class soccer must be played, it should at least be entertaining, and for the most part it was. For one thing, the league adopted a rule — the tiebreaker — to eliminate kissing your sister. The rule, designed to stimulate scoring during games, states that if regulation play produces a tie which is not broken in overtime play, then the teams alternate, taking five penalty kicks each until a winner is decided. In effect for the first time in 1974, the rule put pressure on the players and tension in the stands. It added to the increasing competitiveness of the NASL in a year which saw fouling and fighting increase. In all, the players seemed to be caring more, as though winning in America really did mean something.

The Los Angeles Aztecs, volatile coach and all, won the 1974 championship by defeating none other than the ever-improving Miami Toros, 4-3, on a tiebreaker in the Orange Bowl. CBS televised the game almost nationally (San Francisco and Atlanta didn't carry it) and a vocal crowd of 15,507 attended the game despite 100 degree heat. Los Angeles became the second expansion franchise to win a championship in its first season, duplicating the Atoms' 1973 feat. It was an exciting game, perfect for television, although it captured only a modest 3.8 rating. One negative element, and a glaring one at that, was the absence of American talent. Los Angeles won the championship with no Americans and Miami was runner-up with few Americans on the team.

Where was the American talent? Heavily American-ized teams such as Philadelphia and St. Louis failed to make even the quarterfinals. Superstar Rote led Dallas to a 3-0 quarterfinal win over semi-American San Jose, only to lose 3-1 to Miami in the semifinals. The indication seemed clear enough — if you want to win quick, you need foreign talent. Suddenly, the building blocks so carefully laid by Phil Woosnam seemed precariously balanced. Overseas talent-hunting was increasing in importance again and as 1975 approached, soccer in the U.S.A. seemed to be bending slightly back toward the days of heavy reliance on foreign talent as it did in 1967 and 1968. Now that the sport had captured American interest in some cities, and to a growing extent nationally, would the need to survive in the competitive world of won-loss records again produce soaring expenses, failure to develop American talent, and a loss of fan identification?

Soccer after 1974 was no longer Phil Woosnam's baby; it was a teenager at six years old facing an identity crisis, and it needed some guidance. So Woosnam let his hair grow and prepared to relate.

Phil Woosnam and the butch haircut he favored in his early days as Commissioner of the NASL. *Washington Diplomats photo*.

5.   At the Crossroads

Sonya Strahl, Executive Coordinator and Secretary to the Commissioner, has been with the NASL since 1972 and calls the Commissioner "Phil." Two months before the 1975 season began she took a quick time out to reflect on her years with the league:

"Working here has been extremely fulfilling. It's exciting because each year we grow more and become busier and busier. It's like we're all part of a growing family."

That's what working for soccer in the NASL was like as the 1975 season approached. A family. Still that small, cohesive group, led by Woosnam calling the moves. There had been internal problems every year — folding franchises and the like — but league officials knew how to handle them. After all, the league had stared oblivion in the face in 1969 and avoided it, so any problem seemed small by comparison. Besides, the goals had been clear in the early going — start slowly, become established, cooperate and grow cautiously together, and sell the game to the people. But by early 1975 Woosnam's own plans were taking the NASL out of the elementary stages and into and beyond the intermediate. And there were rumblings in the pit of the NASL; rumblings with American accents.

"This country will become the hub of world soccer," Woosnam was saying confidently in his office. "Economics of the game will force this. In North America sports are promoted better than anywhere in the world. The rest of the world can't keep up with changes that have come in society and new promition angles.

"Twenty four teams will be the upper limit for awhile (there were twenty in 1975), but we'll grow to thirty two soon and certainly forty teams in ten years time."

From these statements, no one will ever accuse Woosnam of thinking small. Woosnam's forty soccer team dream is not based totally on the traditional idea that there's a whole world of talent to choose from. It's a red, white and blue dream based on his hopes that "eventually there will be two to five million boys playing soccer on all levels of competition in this country." To hasten this development, the NASL, according to Woosnam, "agreed to help underwrite the formation of a national team to the extent of $400 thousand." The program, in addition to helping provide for the national team, also is aimed at developing "a coaching system throughout the country to increase coaching ability; the country would be covered by a network of coaches. American stars will develop from a strong national team."

While it's still too early to tell if the NASL has invested its $400,000 wisely, Dettmar Cramer's transatlantic skip out as national team coach certainly put a slight damper on Woosnam's plans. Further complicating the situation has been the shamefully slow permanent appointment of a full time national team coach. Woosnam does not have sole jurisdiction in this area, since he must work with USSF in establishing the coach and team, as he points out, but he's ever the optimist. "We may yet develop a strong national team," he says. "The attitude within the league is to go forward to get a team that can qualify for the World Cup in '78. The passage of time between coaches hasn't hurt the development of the team much because the players have been playing. What we do from August ('75) to August ('76) is what's important."

Woosnam's grand plans seem a little incongruous with his low key demeanor. But, in the infant era of the NASL at least, his record speaks for itself, and the reason for his success was always the carefully calculated analysis of the league's necessities. Such calculations may yet bring about some form of his ultimate design for the league. Each year the financial demands for entering the NASL have grown more stringent; by the start of the 1975 season prospective owners had to meet five basic requirements:

1) Posting a $75,000 performance bond.

2) Financial strength to the tune of half a million dollars over three years.

3) A franchise fee of $100,000. (By 1976, according to Ted Howard, Woosnam's assistant, this fee will come to a total of $350,000 — $100,000 for the actual franchise fee plus relinquishing the rights to $250,000 more.)

4) A proper facility for playing the games.

5) League approval of the financial parties involved and approved by active owners of the new franchise.

Such requirements guarantee a reasonable amount of financial stability to individual franchises. The idea, of course, is to win back some of the monied types lost after '67 and '68 and get a reasonable time and money commitment from them. Three years may not be quite enough time, and the way some of the owners operate a half million dollars may not be quite enough, but it should give teams time to show reason for financial hope — at least, those teams willing to take a logical approach to the selling of the sport.

Amid the red ink that still shows on most soccer team profit and loss ledgers, some black is creeping in. In 1974, the Seattle Sounders, playing in a small but frequently packed stadium, lost a mere $45,000. Barring unforeseen financial troubles, the Sounders were headed for a profit in 1975. So was San Jose, with newcomer Portland also a possibility.

Establishing a team in Seattle, where baseball failed ingloriously after one year, was certainly one of the NASL's best moves, and many teams could well afford to take success lessons from Seattle. The Sounders' 1974 showing prompted expansion of Memorial Stadium from 13,000 capacity in 1974 to 17,426 in 1975. While that size wouldn't suit an NFL team, the Sounders don't have to charge $8.00 or more per ticket to make a profit, so it suits them fine. The Sounders have taken on a whole personality and extended it to the city. In John Best, the Sounders have a coach with promotional sense as well as soccer sense.

"Let's face it, we're selling ourselves out there," says Best, who at thirty five has been a bit-part movie player and magazine model as well as playing soccer for Liverpool and Stockport, England. "We don't just put our people out there and say, 'Come see us.' We went out and talked to people and became visible within the community, so now we have identified with practically the whole community. We let the people see that we're human beings.

"Of course, once people come to the stadium, the product must be good enough to sell itself. And that gets around to one of my pet peeves — negative soccer. We can't afford to play negative soccer in the NASL. We can't just say we're looking for a result so we won't score on anyone, but they sure won't score on us either. This game must be sold with good aggressive offensive soccer.

"When the team first came here I asked the media to just give us a fair shot to entertain and excite people. We did it and the rapport with the crowds out here has been fantastic.

"When I started playing in the United States (in 1967, with the soon defunct Philadelphia Spartans), I met people who didn't want to know me or my teammates because we were foreign and so was soccer. But whenever we were given the chance in clinics or demonstrations we got people, especially kids, to enjoy it and they became more interested. We did essentially the same thing in Seattle by appealing to American Junior League people. We've been given the chance and the crowds here have been very positive. The crowd comes out to lift you here."

Whatever small profit shows in Seattle's books will be there because of logical management. By playing aggressive soccer in a small, but close to full, stadium the feeling of excitement is multiplied. The players in Seattle have been known to do oddly engaging things like throwing roses into the stands, in addition to showing up at soccer clinics and group luncheons for free. Excitement plus team personality have produced strong ticket demand at reasonable prices (over 7,400 season tickets sold for 1975). Pretty soon the bottom line will come up black instead of red.

Still, there are teams and people that have been

around long enough to recognize the right direction, yet balk at it. In Washington, the Diplomats began the 1975 season the way they spent much of 1974 — in a dilemma; only this time it was not completely of their own making. In early May, just six weeks before their opening game, the Diplomats were informed that a new grass surface being installed in RFK Stadium would not be ready in time. Programs, advertising, tickets and brochures already purchased were rendered useless and a lawsuit never got out of the briefcase, since the Diplomats had never in fact signed a contract to use RFK.

What seemed like a tragedy ultimately gave the Diplomats a chance to make some strong fans, and possibly some money.

A suggestion floating around the Washington area that had merit, but was never tried, was for the Diplomats to play half of their games in suburban Virginia and half in suburban Maryland, exposing the pros to those areas where interest is highest. Then, after a couple of years, as quality of play improves and as status of the players and the team rises, move them to RFK.

Pressed for a stadium, the Diplomats contracted one of the largest (12,000 seat) high school stadiums in the area, Woodson High School Stadium in suburban Fairfax, Va. The pressbox was cramped, the field was too small, and the ground sloped just before the out-of-bonds lines. But the parking was free, the location was just right for the nearly 40,000 soccer-playing youngsters in Northern Virginia, and the rental price was low — approximately $1,000 per game as compared to about $5,000 at RFK. For six consecutive home games attendance averaged close to 8,000 per game, and that coincided with a long stretch in May where the popular

Washington Bullets basketball team was involved in the NBA playoffs.

However, the Diplomats were purchased by a new group led by Joseph Danzansky, respected head of a thriving supermarket-department store chain, who switched the remaining games back to RFK. The first game there drew 35,620, but that was for Pelé and the New York Cosmos. For the next two home dates, the Diplomats barely averaged 2,000.

Mike Kossar, in charge of group ticket sales for the Diplomats, said following the switch to RFK, "It's really screwed me up. I had groups that I did $600-$700 or more worth of business with going out to Woodson that I can't do $2.00 with at RFK. They don't want to go all the way into D.C. and pay $2.00 to park in poorly supervised lots."

On the other hand, Danzansky indicated repeatedly that his group was prepared to lose money to play in a major league park. That they had the money was never in doubt. For the Diplomats' franchise, which was bought for $75,000 in 1974, the Danzansky group paid $650,000.

The reason most frequently given about reluctance to use smaller stadiums is that they lack a professional image. Miami Toros coach Greg Meyers, who watches a few thousand people per game swim around the empty seats in the Orange Bowl's 82,000 capacity stadium, admits, "I'd prefer a smaller, 10,000 seat stadium. But I guess there's an aura of first class in the Orange Bowl."

Images aside, the fact is that a club that loses money year after year is not a club at all before long. The stadium identity crisis is a poor reason for a soccer club to go down the drain. Commissioner Woosnam says, "The size and intimacy of the stadium are important," but he considers

105

"quality management, a coach who knows the game, and the open mindedness of the media to the sport" as important or more important than stadium size. He's correct that no matter what the stadium is like, bad personnel on and/or off the field will most likely produce poor attendance. But the fact remains that in areas like stadium rental costs, crowd reaction, and better accessibility for people interested in the game, smaller stadiums with more appropriate locations need greater consideration around the league.

It would seem that economics should overtake image on the issue of stadium size, because, as soccer makes bigtime noises as it did in 1975, it will start making some bigtime economic demands that teams should be ready for.

Comparing the league in 1975 with the league in the late sixties, Woosnam says, "Now there is so much unity that it's just a question of getting the money to make this thing take off. The money will come from within the sport itself. There will be commercial support because the attitude that this is a foreign sport is completely changed now. This sport is becoming the most popular sport in suburbia."

In order to help generate income and avoid squandering thousands of dollars on expensive foreign talent, a $54,000-$60,000 maximum salary per club was supposedly in effect in 1975. Woosnam indicates that there is "no league-prescribed budget," but "owners do discuss budgets among themselves." The resulting total payroll for onfield player personnel (some players supplement it with management level jobs) was the $54,000-$60,000 figure. On an eighteen man team, that is an average of a little over $3,000 per man. That's whip-out cash for the Joe Namath, David Thompson, Catfish Hunter crowd. Similar maximums supposedly were in effect in previous years as well.

The salary budget ceiling may have been an honest enough economic necessity, but it has created some difficulties that are just beginning to surface.

The idea that soccer in the U.S. can be considered of major league caliber at minor league salaries is ludicrous. That it has gotten as much notice as it has under the circumstances is amazing. How many times has a minor league baseball game been televised nationally? How about semipro football? That's what NASL salary figures say their product is, and the low salaries paid make the financial survival chances of teams drawing small crowds to large stadiums all the more difficult. True, the NASL is building and doing a decent job of it; but instead of putting low budget players into high budget stadiums, the procedure should be reversed. Save the money on the stadium rather than on the players. Pay players more, thereby justifying more demands from them in the form of practice and training, and then put the improved product for show at an adequate but less expensive facility. The measure of major league is more what you put on the field than what field you put it on.

For the most part, pro soccer players living year-round in America are part-time professionals, and the salary ceiling helps keep them in that situation. Soccer is usually their moonlighting job since their other occupation is the primary source of income. On the other hand, loan players, players who come to the States for spring-summer soccer but are legally the property of a foreign club, actually have two soccer incomes to draw from — one from their team in their homeland and one from their

American team. If their American club pays $3,000-$4,000 for a season's work, that, combined with their home club's pay, provides a decent way to spend the off season. Americans coming out of college and going into the pros may be carried by the pro club as amateurs at $50-$70.00 per game. In his first full season Kyle Rote Jr. earned $1,400 for his onfield play (but he also held a front office public relations job.) The problem beginning to brew in the league is obvious — if Americans can't make a living at the game, why should they play?

The NASL in 1975 said that each team must carry five American players on its roster. In 1972, the rule was that two Americans must be on the roster, and it was generally believed that each year for the next several years the number would be increased by one. Unfortunately, no rule stating that Americans must be played or how much they must be paid was in existence. Consequently many teams, St. Louis being the most noteworthy exception because of its traditionally high number of Americans, play the loan players more and pay them better since they have superior talent. While the idea that the better you produce the more you get paid makes sense economically and in the won-loss column, the emphasis on loan players is the source of growing agitation around the NASL.

"American players, and soccer in general, can't succeed in the United States with American kids sitting on the bench," says Walter Bahr, Penn State's coach and a leading proponent of rapid Americanization. "The league is making a mistake in its player limitation policy. It should be that teams carry only five foreign players on a squad while the rest are Americans."

Bahr feels his plan would work without sacrificing the quality of play. "The five foreign players could be five

108

good ones," he explains. "The five foreign players could be the team's stars, but the other six positions would be played by Americans who would be gaining valuable experience.

"Nothing's more discouraging than to see American kids sitting on the bench. In the long run the league will lose customers by not playing the local kids."

Bahr points out a problem experienced by his son, Chris, a first year player for the Philadelphia Atoms, as an example of some difficulties faced by young Americans in the NASL. Chris, a three-time All American at Penn State and the Atoms' first-round draft choice for 1975, started for Philadelphia but admits, "college ball wasn't really enough preparation for the pros." His father feels it goes further.

"Foreign players pass the ball to people they know best; it's natural," Walter Bahr claimed early in the 1975 season. Three fourths of the way through the season, following consistent regular play for coach Al Miller's Atoms, Chris Bahr began showing he knows what to do with the ball when he gets it. In one four-game stretch he blasted five goals, proving that there's no better way to improve at the game than by playing it. By the end of the season, Bahr had scored eleven goals and two assists and was named NASL Rookie of the Year.

Another American who proved he had the talent when given the chance to play is Bob Rigby, Atoms goalkeeper and Chris Bahr's teammate. In 1973, Rigby was considered one of the shining examples of the ultimate, dedicated American soccer player — playing for next to nothing while waiting for the sport to explode. Two years later he shows signs of growing impatient, tiring of supplementing his income by substitute teaching.

"The league changes as far as its intentions go every year," Rigby begins. "It was supposed to be concentrating on the development of Americans to play the game. Now, development takes a back seat to team competition. Coaches pay more for foreign players because they feel the foreigners can help them win sooner.

"There should be a limit of five or six top notch foreign players per team. The rest should be Americans. The excuse in the past was that Americans didn't have the talent. But it's just a matter of experience. If given the chance, they could do the job.

"Sure, I'm upset, but I'm probably not as upset as some guys who haven't been given a chance. My income is equivalent with loan players in the league because I do public relations for the team — some of it is boring, but the camps and coaching I enjoy. Like that, I can make a living pretty much.

"Some teams don't adhere to the salary ceilings. The league office is so flexible it's not going to stop or penalize teams. The league can't get too upset because the league must keep going. Right now, the game isn't that concerned with American players.

"I'm just making my living as a goalie. But there are a lot of days when I'd like to get out."

Kyle Rote Jr. has an alternate plan for reversing the imbalance of salaries and roster space between American and loan players. It involves dollars instead of just roster openings.

"Loan players can afford to play for $3,000 or $3,500 and then return to their home country and play there," Rote says, warming to the subject. "In their situation the money's not bad. But players living in the United States can't live on that kind of money.

"There should be a maximum total of $25,000 per team on salaries paid to loan players. If a team wants one at $25,000, or two at $12,500 each, or however they choose to split it, it shouldn't exceed $25,000."

Rote's plan would allow Americans to wrangle with management free of a salary ceiling. It's a plan that would provide more equity and incentive for American players.

The dichotomy existing between NASL objectives and what it wants to pay to reach them has hit coaches especially hard. Charged with the tasks of achieving team unity, developing American talent, promoting the game, and winning, there may be more than a little truth to the claim of Diplomats coach Dennis Viollet that, "The NASL is the hardest league in the world to coach in."

The critical league issues of attendance, salaries, loan players and American players all affect the team, that group of individuals the coach must keep in tune to win. Of course, the way coaches feel about the issues is crucial to the development of the game. Affecting the coaches' feeling is the improving level of competition in the NASL, an improvement virtually every coach has seen from year to year. In fact, there is some fear that league competition is improving too fast, thereby slowing American development while teams struggle to remain competitive, as Rigby pointed out.

. "Right now, the league itself is most important," says Al Miller, coach of the Philadelphia Atoms whose 1973 team was the miracle story of soccer and whose 1975 team, because of injuries and other reasons, was entrenched near last place much of the season. "As far as American players go, we're doing it. More teams are playing them, but it won't happen overnight. When the league is a little more settled, we can begin to limit the number of imports. But we can't do it while we're still expanding; we need players with experience."

Al Miller, it will be remembered, is a native-born American whose championship game lineup in 1973 included six American starters. He cannot be accused of being un-American in his soccer beliefs. He merely shows how the pressure of the rapidly improving league influences a coach's thinking.

However, one team, St. Louis, started its Americanization program in 1969 and each year since then has drawn as much talent as possible from the large, thriving soccer community in St. Louis. John Sewell, coach of the Stars since 1974 and a player for them in '72 and '73, has had to stay competitive by relying on the homegrown brand of player, though he is an Englishman. Seven of his American players have been developing with him for three years, including 1973 when he headed the defense. After a record of 4-15-1 in '74, the Stars spent much of 1975 battling for first place in their division.

Sewell's problems have been compounded by the fact that St. Louis is as sophisticated a soccer audience as can be found in the U.S., and the fans tolerance level for inadequate play is low. However, attendance, while not what it could or should be, especially in 1975, seems supportive enough to keep a team there. Eventually Stars fans may well see their team become the first American soccer superpower because of the management's patient development of Americans.

Sewell admits the development hasn't been easy, especially with the rest of the league bolstering the foreign products. Sewell also uses some topnotch foreigners in key positions, most notably in the goal, where he has English International goalkeeper Peter "The Cat"

Bonetti; but in all, only five Stars were born in a foreign country and two of those five now live in St. Louis year round. The remaining fourteen players on the 1975 Stars roster were born in St. Louis. Sewell's cultivating an American crop, and he feels more of the same throughout the league is vital to the growth of soccer in America.

"Because of the lack of American players in the league, it will take soccer a minimum of ten years to catch on in the U.S.," Sewell believes. "But teams don't want Americans unless they can play like Pele right away. It's hard work developing Americans. In St. Louis we work year round at it.

"The use of loan players must be restricted and incentives for Americans must be increased. It must happen."

If Sewell sounds urgent, he is. And he's not alone. Greg Myers, the young American-born coach of the Miami Toros, is one who shares Sewell's urgency. "We can't go much longer without having a rule to get American kids in the lineup. People will say it will hurt the quality of the game, but we're going to have to take American kids and give them double practice sessions.

"There should be a mandatory rule saying that a certain number of Americans should be in the lineup — on the field playing. If you take one out, put a new one in. That will force pro coaches to pay more attention to them. If we expect American kids to continue practicing, we must make a place for them. We must do it quick because this league will sink or swim with American talent.

"There was a rule for using Americans brought up in the league meetings (winter of '75), and it was voted down. It's unfortunate that the league doesn't take a stronger stand on it.

Bright young stars like Michael Ian Bain, shown here during and after he scored his first professional goal, must be convinced they can make their living at soccer in America. *Photo by Dennis Mallon.*

"The truth of the matter is that American prospects may soon be left behiond the rest of the talent. Americans are not gaining at the same pace as we're bringing in foreigners."

Dennis Viollet, Diplomats' coach who was once quoted as saying he would never use an American just because he was American, is by no means a hardcore anti-Yankee. But he is a realist who knows that winning is synonomous with survival in a coach's vocabulary.

"Teams should be allowed only three players from overseas," Viollet says. "You need them because others can watch them and learn. But bringing in players is good for winning, not for growth and identity."

Again, there's the pressure of winning and the coach's fear that while he's Americanizing and trying to build fan identification, other coaches will play foreigners and beat his brains out. What provisions can be made to satisfy all?

The answer does not come from the league office. While Phil Woosnam is an advocate of increasing the number of American players in the pro game, in the summer of 1975 he was vague about the method and speed of Americanization. When asked what his position would be if a rule specifying how many Americans must be in the game were proposed at off season league meetings, Woosnam said: "That needs careful consideration. There's nothing more embarrassing for a player than to be put in a situation before he's ready for it. The public says, 'We want them (American players) in,' but the public can destroy them.

"I'm not sure how that situation will be handled. I'd like to see a proper farm system organized, but I can't be sure we have the money to support one."

About the possibility of increasing the number of American players on team rosters from five to six, Woossnam said, "That won't be decided until post season meetings. The right formula is just not known at this point. We're looking for a formula which will allow twenty teams to attract enough attendance to stay alive."

Of course, staying alive is paramount in everyone's mind — Woosnam's, players', coaches', and the owners' who vote annually on whether or not to renew Woosnam's contract as commissioner. But the fact that Woosnam was unable, or unwilling, to state his feelings on specific methods of increasing the numbers and playing time of American players is diasppointing. Certainly, as commissioner he is obligated to implement what the owners want; but he should also be a major force in forming policy, as he was in the early days of the league — particularly on such a crucial issue. By not specifying his inclinations, except to give high priority to the obvious — the league's need to stay alive— he risks frustrating the interest of the growing number of American soccer fans and players, from youngsters through pros alike, not to mention coaches inclined to playing some Americans if others will only do the same.

Probably the biggest factor in increasing the number of Americans playing the game will be a couple of titles by a mostly American team like St. Louis. Then other NASL teams may be convinced that Americans can win. But one thing seems certain— if teams want American players who will work twice a day to improve their skill, players who will be assets on and off the field, they'll have to pay for them. There's nothing major league about semi-pro, and, by their salaries and talent, that's exactly what a lot of American soccer players are today. If demands are made to improve their talent, as they should be, then salaries should be adjusted upward accordingly. If the league and individual teams take a positive stance toward this, soccer may be able to avoid the messy, image-marring financial struggles athletes and owners in other sports have had. To soccer players looking for a chance to survive as professional athletes, money is a huge incentive. However, the area of salary improvement, ever a painful subject, already causes some hedging in soccer circles.

When talking of salaries, Woosnam begins dusting off cliches. He speaks carefully, euphemistically, and painfully realistically.

"As much as we'd like to see respectable salaries, it will take a few years yet. The game can't support it now. I honestly believe there's nothing wrong in players playing on a part-time basis and having another occupation. It's good for them because one of the major problems in professional sports is that palyers take up the sport and come to the end of their career with more responsibility, and they're not adequately prepared to go out into life at that time.

"We're very appreciative of what players have done. They really have become missionaries. One day they will look with envy at what players are earning. But no players will ever have the sense of satisfaction and gratitude from people as the ones who were in during these difficult five years where they put their shoulder to the wheel and played their hearts out. I'm sure they've enjoyed it."

Indeed, many players indicate their love of the game is so great they would play for nothing. "People play because they like the game, so money isn't a factor for a lot of guys." admits Bob Rigby. That, coupled with very real pioneer motivation and a good outside job, has kept non-loan players in the U.S. relatively happy for several years. But before long, those days may become just so much nostalgia; and as they fade, soccer in the U.S.A. will come closer to becoming a truly professional major league sport.

On the horizon is the surest sign that the NASL will soon be haggling with players over tangibles like salaries, insurance and retirement benefits (the league has nothing established in the latter two areas). A Soccer Players' Association (SPA) is in its formative stages, and before soccer fans cringe at the thought, they should understand that given the current state of the sport in America, such an organization could be beneficial to the whole game. The most important thing it could do intially is to allow for a players' voice in developmental aspects of the game like the national team, training óf Americans, and use of Americans. If well received and properly used, an SPA could become an important stabilizing force for pro soccer players.

Currently spearheading the organization of an SPA is Kyle Rote Jr., biggest American name in soccer, whose neck is stuck out furthest in SPA talks.

"We're not trying to organize in order to strike," Rote is quick to point out, since he is acutely aware of what he calls the "negative public view of sports unions."

"We really don't have any strike potential anyway at present, since there's a whole world full of soccer players to draw from. Right now, we're mainly concerned with improving communications among players, and from players to the commissioner's office."

Rote's philosophy on SPA operations is conservative at present, based on his hopes that once communications between players and owners improve, changes beneficial to both groups will come naturally. The possibility concerns Rote that some players will "come on too strong and press too hard in certain areas" once the SPA is operative. He indicates he would not support such actions in the association's early stages, though he understands why players might support a hardline approach from the start.

"So many players in this league have been lied to by owners," Rote says. "The owners tell some guys they can't pay them over a certain amount because of league rules, but then they turn around and pay a loan player the higher amount. Owners say they can't provide cars or apartments, but they do for some guys, mainly loan players."

The SPA will probably have some membership problems even following expected approval as a bargaining unit by the National Labor Relations Board, because as Bob Rigby, a supporter of the SPA concept fears, "I doubt if foreign players will go along with it."

The possibility, then, is that friction will develop between the pro-SPA group, who will view the organization as a move toward professionalism, and the anti-SPA group, comprised primarily of loan players who will see it as possibly destroying their summers of fun and profit. In all, it will make for a pretty hot family squabble.

The league is making one major move toward providing more soccer playing experience, and more money for owners and players alike, by moving the game indoors in the winter. By altering the rules a little, cutting the number of participating players from 11 to six, providing indoor artifical turf, squashing the goal to four feet high, and allowing players to pass the ball off the boards, the game adapts well to indoor facilities.

In the confines of, say, Philadelphia's Spectrum, soccer becomes a more compact, physical game played for the fans in close-to-the-action surroundings. Goals are scored more rapidly than outdoors and everyone's moves must be quicker. During the winter of 1975, the NASL put on an indoor tournament that included sixteen clubs and received some national television coverage from CBS. It was just an experiment, but it received immediate favorable reviews.

George Beahon of ABC-TV in Rochester, N.Y. predicted on the air after watching an indoor game, "The sport will go big time in big city markets. It is made to order for television . . . more so than lacrosse, tennis, hockey or even basketball. It will become the biggest thing on the commercial tube since pro football."

Such praise of the indoor game is not new. A year earlier, following indoor soccer's Philadelphia debut in a game between the Atoms and the touring Russian Army team which drew 11,790 to the Spectrum, Ray W. Kelly of the Camden, New Jersey *Courier-Post* wrote in a column headlined "Six a Side Proves More Like Homicide".

"Imagine one of those schoolyard basketball games where every bucket comes on a fast break. Mix in a little hockey-type board-checking. And add a pinch of dodgeball.

"Now make the use of hands illegal and you've got six-a-side . . . "

1975's indoor tournament was just a brief test to see how the game would be received, and it seems to have passed the test at least in Woosnam's mind. "We may expand the tournament next year (winter of 1976) and have league play in two years," Woosnam says. He sees the indoor season as a device for satisfying, as he puts it, "the need to play nine months and sixty games per year."

Since indoor play is still in its early stages, it has some rough edges for teams to deal with. Scheduling, for example, will conflict in many cities with basketball and hockey, meaning the game may be forced into some less than prime dates. Rentals for indoor facilities may prove a strain on some team budgets, depending upon which part of the 2,500 to 11,000 plus 1975 attendance range teams fall in.

Also, a method for keeping basically the same players on indoor and outdoor rosters for purposes of fan identification must be established. Since loan players will be off in their home countries playing the outdoor game, American players will have a chance to sharpen their skills in the indoor version. However, if a team plays its indoor games, with a vastly different roster than it plays its outdoor games, separate groups of fans are likely to develop — those preferring the indoor team and game, and those preferring the outdoor team and game. Such fragmentation could prove disastrous diluting public interest in soccer instead of strenghtening it.

In 1975 the outdoor game received the greatest amount of public support ever in the NASL. Pelé-inflated league attendance, which rose to an averae of nearly 8,000 per game, and competition between teams reached all time highs. There were five new franchises — San Antonio, Chicago, Portland, Tampa Bay and Hartford. By mid-season the Portland Timbers and Tampa Bay Rowdies were showing good drawing power while the Chicago Sting and San Antonio Thunder flirted with the 5,000 range, in attendance and league play.

Prior to the season, when asked why Hartford was

awarded a franchise, NASL Director of Administration Ted Howard explained, "There's strong traditional interest in soccer there. It's a growing franchise, one of the top TV markets, and the World Hockey Association is there." Unfortunately for the Hartford club, the knowledgeable fans saw all too well that a team with a leaky defense and a low-scoring offense would not win much. Hartford, which plays in a sensibly sized 14,000 seat stadium, is one of those teams that will have to produce a winner quickly to attract the traditionalists.

Watching NASL pro soccer in 1975 was really a study in contrasts. On the teams were players who, for the most part, would have only an outside chance of being first or even second division caliber in Europe, competing earnestly while the league tried to arouse interest. At the same time the problems of undersized crowds, oversized stadiums, underpaid players and underplayed Americans gnawed at the sport. Yet on the field the feeling of being part of a team took over, as it does in any team sport, and the players became performrers concerned with winning and providing excitement.

The scene could be anywhere in the NASL in 1975, but let's focus on Dallas, one of the two remaining charter NASL franchises, to capture the atmosphere of a single NASL game.

As members of the Tornado team gather in the tunnel prior to taking the field in Texas Stadium, the players exhibit the emotions typical to athletes going to work. Some strain to laugh at forced jokes. Others are quiet, intent pictures of concentration. Still others mutter quick, quiet, brief comments as they shrug their shoulders or stretch their legs or twist their trunks attempting to fight tension. Team captain Roy Evans gets them organized in the tunnel, clapping his hands and urging, "C'mon, lads," to a couple of teammates arriving late from the trainer's table. A few shouts of encouragement, a burst of isolated handclapping, and on cue from the announcer, each Tornado trots onto the field.

The starting eleven all carry plastic orange and royal blue panelled soccer balls onto the field. Each starter kicks his ball into the stands where hopeful youngsters scramble for it. One Tornado's first kick falls short of the stands; so, showing slight embarrassment, he retrieves the ball and makes good on his second attempt to the good natured applause of the hometown fans.

Barely one tenth of the 65,000 royal blue seats of Texas Stadium are filled and the announcer's comments are nearly inaudible because of the echo. Many of the fans are teenage or younger, and they cheer most enthusiastically at contact resulting from close marking and at nearly every ball that is headed. Fine points like Mickey Moore's excellent dribbling in a crowd do not receive as much response. But then, finesse is often difficult for the inexperienced to appreciate.

The crowd reacts loudly when the smallish (five-nine, 153 pound) Moore is elbowed, pushed, and run over by a much larger opponent. Moore responds with typical competitiveness, but he's overpowered and on one play he is knocked to the ground. Carpet burns from the artificial turf redden Moore's knees and thighs. He's the crowd's favorite for the time being and the fans let him know it be encouraging Moore to "Kill him!"

Dallas' offense has difficulty sustaining an attack, a problem the team faced throughout the year, keeping the Tornado defense under constant pressure. On the sidelines, Dallas Coach Ron Newman begins to show the strain of facing a possible loss. "Referee, referee! The ball goes our way you deaf bastard," he yells in exasperation. But neither Newman's shouts, nor the team's efforts, nor the crowd's pleading can turn the game around. Dallas loses, 2-0.

Burns, bruises and disappointment are obvious on the players in the Tornado dressing room. A few autograph seekers wait impatiently outside, and a security guard unfortunately chooses to indirectly insult the Tornado when he responds to a question by saying loudly in a mocking tone, "I can't help you. I don't know these Tornado officials like I do the Cowboy officials."

Following the game, about 200 members of the Tornado Boosters Club mill around the Stadium Club inside Texas Stadium. They eat, drink, and dance to live music, and make small talk with Tornado players who mix with the crowd for about an hour and then leave for home. The next morning means work for most of them.

So it went. A surreal season. An aura of the big time amid small time salaries and recognition. But there was excitement for those within the sport and for those who followed it closely.

The NASL point system — six points for a win, none for a loss, and one point for each goal scored up to three per game — encouraged offensive play and also made division races closer. Late in the season teams with just average won-loss records still had a chance to make the playoffs because of the point system. Consequently, they bore down and focused on getting the maximum of nine points (six for winning, one for each goal socred up to three per game) to close the gap on their opponents.

Around the league nearly every team experienced good, bad, hope, despair, luck, and misfortune at varying points during the season. Miami's speeding forward from Trinidad, Steve David, illustrated how coach Greg Myers' offense minded play should work by spending much of the summer on a scoring rampage. In one game he scored five goals, a league record. But the high spirited Toros, plagued by injuries and suspensions for fighting, sputtered late in the season, though David went on to score 23 goals and six assists for 52 points en route to winning the NASL's Most Valuable Player award.

In Baltimore, the Comets spent much of the year holding on tenaciously to last place in the Eastern Division, but with five games left in the season Al Collins, Comets' general manager, replaced Doug Millward as coach. Taking his soccer personality (intense) and philosophy (score) to the Baltimore coaching job, one of the league's most hapless offensive teams began scoring and winning. What's more important to soccer in general, and Baltimore in particular, are Collins' attitudes toward the game in America.

Regardless of what the rest of the league does, Collins says, "Each year we'll (the Comets) add American players. In three to four years it's my ambition to have a good American team here. While my team won't win a championship right away, we'll gain experience from playing with teams loaded with foreigners and we'll win eventually.

"When I took over as coach I told my foreign players, 'You're here to help your American teammates learn the game.' So they helped me teach the basics.

"The league shold raise the minimum number of Americans on the teams from five to nine or ten. Then you'd have to play some of them. That's what will help this game draw more — fans could watch the Americans improve each year. But it'll take a lot of guts from the owners and coaches, particularly those with teams already loaded with foreigners."

Collins has the guts, but he may not have the team. Persistent rumors in 1975 had the Comets, who averaged on the shy side of 3,000 in attendance all year, making like a lawnchair and folding. If that happens it would be unfortunate, given Collins' plans and the staidum located in suburban Towson at Towson State College. In 1974 the Comets played in oversized (45,000 soccer capacity) Memorial Stadium in downtown Baltimore and drew poorly despite finishing in the playoffs. In 1975 the Comets moved to suburbia but did not play well. Perhaps if they could put their 1974 season in their 1975 stadium, with a high number of American players, the elements of good team, good location, and Americanization would bolster attendance. With a little more promotional imagination, the strong natural rivalries between Baltimore, Philadelphia, and Washington could be played up to draw fans. But the financial burden may snuff out these possibilities and Al Collins' noble plans.

The Comets could take some solace in the fact that in 1975 none of the Eastern Division's other veteran teams could catch the expansion franchise Tampa Bay Rowdies either. Combining creative promotions with winning soccer, the Rowdies began attracting low five-figure crowds to Tampa Stadium after a slow start. Members of the Rowdies were all over the Tampa community drumming up support. Players spoke to hundreds of community organizations, marched in parades while kicking soccer balls, and coached thousands of area youth. Besides having an active sounding nickname,

Tampa also came up with a most engaging slogan: "Soccer is a Kick in the Grass!"

Much of the same approach used by Tampa also contributed to the onfield and ticket office success of the Western Division's expansion club, the Portland Timbers. Playing in perhaps the best overall division of the NASL, the Timbers made ready for league play by signing six loan players from England's first division, ranging in age from nineteen to twenty-three. Playing in comfortably sized (26,000 seats) Civic Stadium, Portland showed again that if a competitive expansion club extends itself to the community and plays in suitable surroundings, it can enjoy good attendance. The Timbers were attracting 17,000-18,000 regularly by July when they overtook Seatttle for the division lead and headed for a playoff berth.

Portland showed good promotional sense by agreeing to compete against Vancouver for the Columbia Cup, a championship award for the annual winner of the season's series between the two teams. Portland won the cup in 1975 by defeating the Whitecaps in all three regular season games. The cup spurred attendance, and will take on more significance as the rivalry between the two teams grows stronger with time.

The Seattle Sounders established what should become a trend, by forming a B team to play exhibitions against local college and club teams. The B team will give Seattle reserves and less experienced players a chance to work on their skills, and offers another means of establishing fan rapport. The Sounders continued to play winning soccer and their fan support was perhaps the most intense in the league.

There were uncertain teams too, like Washington: uncertain about who would own them, who would promote them, where they would play, and who would play, the Dips had a quality about them that only Washington fans could love. In a town loaded with smooth but shifty politicos, slap-your-back-while-I-twist-your-arm lobbyists, and a pro football team with a full time security guard who looks for spies while riding a bicycle during practice, the Diplomats were refreshingly down to earth.

Not that they didn't try to be first class and suave. In fact, at times they succeeded. But Washington's grown used to that, so it was their mishaps that were appealing.

There was the Ordering of the Goal Posts episode which stemmed from a misunderstanding about where the team's practice site would be. Seems someone from the Dips' front office thought he had secured a local motel/country club as the training site, complete with privileges to use the entire facility. The only problem was that the area of land where the practice field was to be did not have any goalposts, so the Dips immediately ordered a set. Just prior to beginning practices the Dips discovered that the person at the motel/country club who had given them permission to work out there had no real authority to do so. Consequently, the Dips had to find a new practice site. No problem — until mid July when the Dips got a call from the lobby of the building their main office is in, saying there were two official soccer goalposts taking up space. Last word had a Diplomats official trying to haul the posts home in the back of his station wagon.

There was the Problem of the Announcer's Priorities. This example of what not to say during a game occurred with about seven minutes remaining in a hard-played first half against Toronto. As the two teams were at the peak of their intense competition and the crowd of nearly 8;000 was cheering nearly every kick, the announcer said in his richest pearshaped tones, "Folks we have a great halftime show lined up for you this evening so be sure and buy your Diplomats souvenirs now so you won't miss it!" To which a fan responded by looking at the announcer's booth and saying sarcastically, "And I though we were here to see this soccer game."

And there was the Bermuda Angle. Randy Horton, one of the all time leading scorers in the NASL whom the Dips acquired in a preseason trade, provided the drama here. Horton, an assistant headmaster for a shcool in Bermuda, commuted from Bermuda to Washington on game days. Only, by the start of the Toronto game, he hadn't showed up; his flight had been delayed by a storm. The Diplomats played the entire first half without him and without scoring. Horton showed up just in time to start the second half, assisted on the tying goal and scored the winner as the Dips triumphed, 2-1.

If the Dips epitomized the ups and downs of a season, they also epitomized teams with reason to be hopeful. They have a strong suburban following, a new wealthy respected group of owners, and a personable coach in Dennis Viollet, who kept his injury-riddled team in contention for a playoff berth throughout the season. If the club's officials would take a few cues from Seattle, St. Louis and Tampa Bay, the Dips could easily fill Washington's gaping summertime sports void.

The 1975 NASL season ended with a flourish.

Division races were in doubt through the final week of the season with Chicago losing out to Los Angeles for one wild card birth by one total point and Washington missing a playoff shot by two total points to Toronto. The Western Division continued to dominate in attendance with Seattle, Portland, San Jose, Los Angeles and St. Louis all hosting either sellout crowds or crowds of 10,000 or better during the season's final weeks.

Division winners were Boston in the North, Tampa Bay in the East, St. Louis in the Central and Portland in the West. Wild card spots went to Toronto, Miami, Seattle, and Los Angeles. In general the playoffs involving these eight teams showed new strength both on the field and at the gate for the NASL. The Portland-Seattle quarterfinal, won by and played in Portland, set a league playoff record by drawing 31,523 in the soccer crazed Pacific northwest. In other quarterfinal action, Tampa Bay snuck past Toronto 1-0 before 16,111 faithful in Tampa, St. Louis beat Los Angeles 2-1 before a disappointing crowd of 6,119 in St. Louis, and Miami beat Boston 2-1 in overtime before a measly 2,187 in Boston.

The semifinals pitted season-long enemies Miami and Tampa in Tampa and the great American hope St. Louis Stars against the Portland Timbers in Portland. Tampa's Rowdies stifled the Toros 3-0 to the delight of a club record crowd of 22,710 and the Stars succumbed to Portland 1-0 in front of yet another NASL playoff record crowd of 33,503. The victories by Portland and Tampa set up a championship game which would mean that, for the third year in a row, an expansion team would win the title.

While the NASL delights in pointing out the success of expansion teams, it is also a sign of weakness that some of the established clubs have not grown strong enough to eliminate the newcomers. It also means that new teams are bringing in better talent, which is fine except that most of it is foreign.

The NASL's Soccer Bowl '75 was held in San Jose, a city which was highly likely to provide a sellout crowd although its own team, the Earthquakes had finished last in the Western Division during regular season play. The fans did not disappoint the league, as over 18,000 showed up to see Tampa shut out Portland 2-0 in a game characterized by a rather disorganized first half and a well played second half.

Unfortunately, by making San Jose the site of the championship game nearly a year in advance, the NASL deprived the very worthy fans in Portland and Tampa of the opportunity to see the team they supported so well play in one home stadium or the other. Not only that, but the game would probably have drawn at least 4,000 more in Tampa and close to 15,000 more in Portland. Of course, advance planning undoubtedly played an important part in the league's decision, but in future years every effort should be made to play the championship game before the home crowd of a team in the final game.

On the American success side, St. Louis Stars coach John Sewell was named Coach of the Year for piloting his club to a 13-9 season and the Central Division title, scoring points for steady Americanization. Chris Bahr of the Philadelphia Atoms wound up the season with 11 goals and 2 assists to win Rookie of the Year honors.

Naturally, public reaction is vital to soccer. If the people won't pay to see the game, the NASL might as well pull down its goalposts and quietly fade into extinction. Consequently, capturing the public's attention and establishing league credibility have been major concerns of the NASL since the beginning of the Woosnam era in 1969. It has been a delicate road, attempting to maintain a reasonable sense of direction while trying to establish belief in the future of the sport. In general, things seemed to break right for soccer, partly by plan and partly by accident. Today, while it still rarely gets major coverage in the mass media, the general public knows soccer is out there — it is definitelyspreading from the ethnic pockets of urban centers and manufacturing towns, which confined it for so much of the first three quarters of the twentieth century, to white collar suburbia where the foreign label is gradually being removed.

While pro soccer in 1975 hungered for media recongition as a major league, moved toward record attendance, and began acting like a credible sport and business, it lacked the money, talent and fan identification to completely capture the public. The sport faced a classic problem in image building — how to pursue and image with enough substance to accurately reflect reality. If the image is too far removed from reality, credibility is lost.

As the sport moved from the big cohesive family to the colder but more realistic business relationship, it needed something to show the people that would make them believe in the league. It needed an image relecting growth and power. As Phil Woosnam himself believes, "Every sport needs an image to be successful. It's all an image situation." From 1969 through 1974 the small strides like changes in league structure, new franchises, the westward movement, increasing attendance figures, reduced overall financial losses and the like were enough to reflect what soccer wanted — an image illustrating limited but stable growth. But not for 1975, when the league felt the need to show the public and the mass media a more meaningful image to take it from the realm of a growing sport to an arrived sport. But in the areas of quality play, profit and loss, salaries, attendance and mass recognition at the pro level, the NASL came up short.

Woosnam hinted at where the image would be found as he sat in his office in the winter of 1975, and began talking excitedly of his plans for the next few years. Woosnam rearely shows much more emotion than a smiling computer during an interview, not having the time or the inclination to deal in pipedreams or other frivolous matters. His optimism is calculated. So his comments on the game's image were tinged with excitement stemming from confidence about what was to come when he said:

"I'd like to see just a few superstars from the world some day come into this league. Others will benefit more by seeing great players play than from all the words in the world and all the books.

"If you watch a Pelé play and play alongside him; you're going to become a better player. We'll go through a stage of bringing in some of the great players of the world in the next decade. We will then, no doubt, be recognized as the major league in the world.

"If we bring in one per club for thirty two clubs and we have the best thirty two from out there in addition to all our great players ourselves, we'll be a league to be reckoned with.

"We'll bring in the outside players as a means to an end — to raise our standards up to a point where we won't need the outsiders anymore.

"We're trying to capture all the experience, all the skill, and the know how the other people have had a hundred years to develop, and we want to get it all in the next ten years. Then there comes a time when you shut it all off after they've played out their careers. Then you say, Our boys are going to develop their own talents now."

The image was imported from Brazil. But the reality lives in Dallas.

Smaller stadiums like Woodson High School where the Diplomats averaged 8,000 fans per game are easier to fill, cheaper to rent, and provide more atmosphere than larger ones. *Photo by Dennis Mallon.*

When you talk about Pelé you break out a box labelled "Superlatives" and roll out all the euphemisms. When Pelé plays he makes straight news coverage obsolete. Pelé never jumps, he always soars; he never runs, he always darts; he never outhustles opponents, he victimizes them; he never kicks, he always blasts; he is never led, he always leads.

Pelé and the litany of superhuman accomplishments which follows him signed a three year contract totalling $7,000,000 on June 10, 1975, to play soccer for the New York Cosmos of the NASL. Immediately, the superlatives hit the press.

Pelé once caused fighting forces in Biafra to stop fighting long enough to watch him play.

Pelé blasts a ball over a defender's head and darts around him to field it before the man even moves.

Pelé dribbles the ball between the legs of defenders and then blasts in a shot victimizing them again.

Pelé's final goal in international competition was such a beauty that all the bedazzled goalkeeper could do was bow as the shot screamed by.

Pelé wears two pairs of shorts when he plays so in case the crowd rips off one pair (as has happened) he won't be left in his birthday suit.

Pelé has stud value; when his son Edinho was just four years old, the Corinthians Club of Sao Paulo, Brazil, attempted, and failed, to sign him up for $12,000.

Pelé is a movie and TV star in Brazil, playing in a weekly private eye series.

Pelé is better known throughout the world than Larry Csonka, Johnny Bench, Wilt Chamberlain, Gerald Ford, Carol Burnett, and Frank Sinatra.

Pelé is humble, proud, honest, personable, refreshing as a soft drink on a hot day, and one hulluva provider for his wife and two children.

In all, Pelé seems like a pretty good guy. He is definitely one of the best rags-to-riches stories of all time, coming form the small town of Tres Coracoes (Three Hearts), rising to a national hero at sixteen, and becoming an internationally idolized Brazillionair by his mid-twenties.

Pele shows a flair for the charismatic in what he says and does. When he scores a goal, he soars into the air and punches at space — a salute which he made famous in 1957. Following his final game, played before 120,000 spectators in Rio's Maracana Stadium, he yanked off his hallowed jersey no. 10 and took a last lap around the field as his countrymen went wild. Politicians all over the U.S.A. would like to know how Pelé still gets crowd reaction by forming the now supposedly antiquated V sign with his fingers. For Pelé it bring applause; for pols it brings guffaws.

. Pelé left soccer on October 2, 1974, the tears streaming down his face mirroring those shed by his countrymen. Pelé entered the circus on June 10, 1975, the smile on his face mirroing those aound the NASL.

It was a simple enough idea, a publicity stund P.T. Barnum would envy. So you think soccer in the U.S.A. doesn't pay much, eh? What's a $7 million package including a suite of offices, peanuts? So you think the media's going to ignore soccer, eh? So why did CBS jump at the chance to televise Pelé's first game in the States, a mere exhibition against Dallas, nationally and throughout various parts of the world, because they thought no one would watch it? Pelé signed the contract, that's what did it and now people will pay attention. So went the line of thinking.

It almost worked, except Pelé overshadowed the sport. The charisma of Pelé was too far removed from the reality of soccer in the U.S.A., so he became the show while the rest of the league became the supporting cast. But it was quite a show.

From his first press conference as a member of the Cosmos, Pelé became the center of soccer attention. Where in the past if one television camera showed up for a soccer news conference it was parctically deserving of a nationwide press release from the NASL offices, 14 camera crews jammed the Hunt Room of the 21 Club in Manhattan and within 24 hours Pelé was well on the way to becoming a household name and face in the U.S. He broke into the heartland in hours, while soccer itself had waited for years. Pelé was an event in himself, and newsmen literally fought with one another to ask a question, take a picture, or zoom in for a close-up.

Pelé's professional debut as a player in the NASL took place on national TV on June 15, in a quickly organized exhibition against the Dallas Tornado in dilapidated Downing Stadium, home of Pelé and the rest of the New York Cosmos. 21,278 showed up and cheered the league's most valuable player (in the bank if not on the field). Television coverage, which interrupted play often enough to make the game seem like an interruption for non-stop commercials, was terrible but it was economically and psychologically important to soccer. Pelé scored on a classic header, jumping (he did not appear to soar) straight up and, exhibiting precise timing and body control, tilted his body back quickly and then sharply forward, hitting the ball squarely with his head. It was a good shot; excellent form; a lot of velocity. Okay, it blasted into the net. Okay, he did lead the Cosmos to a 2-2 comeback tie. It was definitely the Pelé Show.

Tornado Kyle Rote Jr., reflecting on the exhibition, says, "I discovered what it must feel like to be one of the Washington Generals playing against the Harlem Globetrotters. You're just supposed to be there so there's someone else on the field.

"Pelé showed outstanding leadership in that first exhibition. He dictated where the players should run. But it was obvious he wasn't in very good shape at the time. His ability on the soccer field, of course, is immense, but I'm much more impressed with his ability to handle fame."

Three days later, in his first official league game, Pelé packed Downing Stadium to 22,500, a complete sellout, while 5,000 cars were turned away. The Cosmos won, 2-0, over Toronto, and typically, Pelé was given credit for leading though he did not score a goal.

It would be on the road where Pelé's value would really be tested. The league was counting on him filling parks around the country, giving nearly every team the opportunity for a big pay day and the chance to expose nearby residents to the game. For this privilege host teams averaged what their gross receipts had been for games before the Pelé visit, and then paid the Cosmos 50 percent of whatever Pelé helped them gross over that amount. To share the wealth they shared the cost, so the higher the gross for a Pele game the better it was for everyone.

Road problems developed right away. Pelé's first game as a Cosmos away from New York was played against the Boston Minutemen in 15,000 seat Nickerson field on the campus of Boston University. A standing room only crowd estimated at 25,000 showed up ringing the field. It resulted in a potentially ugly night with Pelé being carried off the field on a stretcher. But the stage had been set earlier and the results were ominous of what Pelé, the image, means to soccer in America.

The Boston episode began building nearly two weeks earlier when the Minutemen pulled a major, but largely unnoticed, soccer coup by signing Eusebio, a Portuguese star whose talents were once widely compared to Pelé's but who never achieved the level of idol internationally. Boston signed Eusebio to a contract after an American Soccer League team botched up a $100,000 deal with him. The Minutemen signed him hoping to attract the large Portuguese speaking segment of the city to Nickerson Field. He was making his debut at his home, after two uninspiring road games, on the night of the Pelé visit. So Eusebio was taking a back seat to Pelé again. But there were other problems, too.

Eusebio had not played well on the road, nor had his signing brought a flood of requests for season tickets. It was later discovered that internal problems were developing. "The players are really put off at Eusebio's big contract," admitted Fred Klashman, director of public relations for the Minutemen. "I'm getting crap from up top because I'm supposedly not pushing Eusebio. He's been profiled in the paper, but I'm thinking about getting him caught in a Playboy club or something. People want a human personality. He hasn't really caught on."

There were rumblings that at 32-years old Eusebio was too slow. One club official described the situation with Eusebio as "miserable", indicating that members of the team felt him undeserving of the fruitful contract he had signed.

There was a lot on the line when Eusebio and Pelé met at Nickerson field. The crowd sensed the tension between the two men and when Eusebio scored in the second half on a direct free kick following a foul by Pelé, the partisan home crowd responded appropriately. But Pelé does not like to be outdone. In a matter of minutes he scored what everyone thought was the tieing goal. Carried away by the drama, the crowd charged Pelé. By most accounts, including Pelé's, the crowd was not hostile. It had reacted more out of a swelling admiration for Pelé's excellent sense of drama. Pelé was soon covered by fans who may have been admiring souvenier hunters, but who were nevertheless inflicting pain as they grabbed, wrenched, twisted and clawed for a momento. Pelé's personal bodyguard, Pedro Garay, and assorted security personnel dispersed the crowd and placed Pelé on a stretcher to the horror of the spectators. Rumors ranged from Pelé having been seriously injured to the whole stretcher scene being a ploy to keep the crowd back. It turned out to be a minor injury to his knee, but the Cosmos played the rest of the game without Pelé and lost 2-1. The goal that caused all the commotion had been disallowed because Pelé had pushed off on the play, a

The young American, Roy Willner of the Washington Diplomats, versus the superstar Legend, Pelé, at RFK Stadium in Washington, D.C. The Legend won, scoring two goals and two assists. *Photo by Dennis Mallon.*

Pelé spins a little magic which causes defenders Brian Pillinger and Roy Willner to collide as the master trots around to the ball. *Photo by Dennis Mallon.*

foul that few had paid attention to at the time. The Cosmos protested the game to the league on the grounds that Boston's inadequate security measures prevented the Cosmos from playing the whole game with a full squad.

Members of the Cosmos organization, notably general manager Clive Toye, were angered over what they considered a lack of security and a deliberate overselling of the stadium. Toye let it be known around the league that adequate security measures would have to be guaranteed Pelé in the future, or the Brazilian legend might just not play. On the other hand, the Minutemen felt the Cosmos were playing up the events at Boston's expense.

"We got hate mail over the Pelé game," claimed Fred Clashman. "New York overplayed things and loved every minute of it. Toye loved every minute of publicity he got from the Pelé injury. Toye complained aboaut inadequate protection, but he had hot property getting mobbed, and he loved it."

What Toye and the Cosmos definitely did love was that Pelé was not seriously injured and that Woosnam upheld their protest, allowing the Cosmos to replay the game. "I felt it was a legitimate protest because not enough security precautions were taken," Woosnam says. "Consequently, New York wasn't allowed to play the complete game with a full squad; they were forced to play without Pelé on the field."

The result was that Boston hosted the make-up game on August 3 at Nickerson Field. Much of the drama, however, was missing since Pelé was out of the Cosmos line-up with a muscle pull.

Exactly how big a setback to the Minutemen the upheld protest was is debatable. The team received national publicity plus the chance to have two big Pelé-inspired pay days, although it didn't work out that way, while many teams were unable to host Pelé even once, a fact which caused some agitation around the league.

"The league should have made a format, to give every team a shot at having Pelé to help attendance," says Al Collins of Baltimore, whose Comets went Pelé-less at home, expressing a wish shared in other cities where attendance lagged.

The Woosnam decision on the Cosmos protest also raised eyebrows belonging to coaches who wondered how the commissioner would rule if their star player suffered the same fate. Woosnam may have set a troublesome precedent for himself in what he calls "strictly a judgement case." Should cases involving other players arise, how will "enough security precautions" be measured? In a game not involving Pelé, is one police officer enough or one hundred? How severely injured does a player have to be; couldn't a club, following commotion by fans, say a player was injured and call for a protest? Does it have to be a star player; if so, how is star measured? Does the injury have to be the result of a crowd, or could it be caused by just one overzealous admirer who unintentionally injures his favorite palyer while trying to embrace him?

So the problem of how to handle the image surfaced early. Clearly, the league moved to protect its investment. Surely, it would be tragic if Pelé were seriously injured bcause of neglected security. No one in soccer is ignorant of his enormous appeal. However, if the image is set too far apart from reality, then soccer will lose credibility. Is the NASL a Pelé exhibition or is it a major league?

"Pelé is the greatest sportsman of all time in all

143

sports," Woosnam proclaims. "He is also a humble, tremendous person. There is no greater missionary for our game. I felt he would produce a favorable reaction, but it far exceeded expectations.

"He provides identification. The image of the sport improves with him. He's attracted the attention of people who now know of soccer."

Well, they know of Pelé anyway.

When Pelé hit Washington on Saturday, June 28, he went to Pennsylvania Avenue in the morning and frolicked in the White House rose garden with that old American footballer, President Ford. Pelé headed a few, dribbled a few, and politely applauded the President's game but clumsy efforts to do the same. The brief meeting between the two world leaders was cordial and they agreed that future talks should be held, Pelé's schedule permitting. Weekend news programs throughout the nation carried film clips of the meeting, and Sunday papers had some nice, causual photographs of the two to choose from. It was the kind of publicity you expect when you pay $7 million.

A general news conference to meet Pelé was arranged by the Washington Diplomats for 3:00 p.m. that same Saturday at the Channel Inn in Washington. The night before, in Rochester, Pelé blasted his first official goal in a 3-0 Cosmos win before a less than capacity crowd of 14,000 ("Remember, that's not bad in Rochester," says a Diplomats official) under beefed-up security. In organizaing the press conference, the Diplomats and Cosmos have taken many pains to avoid a repeat of the New York press conference brawl. In addition to uniformed police, seven plainclothes detectives and Cosmos security men were on hand to insure order. (Was

144

there really a C.I.A. man in the swimming pool posing as a life guard?)

The gentlemen of the press filed into the conference room like children at a school assembly as the Diplomats director of public relations, Jon Rose, assumes the unusual role of a master sergeant. "People with tape recorders first, then reporters with notebooks and then photographers," he barks. Once inside, a few mischievious photographers try to slither closer to the platform where Pelé will appear, but Rose catches them — "Photo people, please do not come to the front", Sgt. Rose rebukes. "Photographers stay on the sides and in the back." The photographers retreat.

Pelé is fashionably late and the waiting reporters take turns joking and bitching about the security. Pelé will speak from a podium in the front of the room which is roped off from the media. "I bet he rises from a platform beneath the floor," quips one reporter. "Don't crack jokes," warns another. "That chandelier sends everything you say to police headquarters."

Either the trumpet fanfare was not cued or it wasn't planned, but Pelé walks onto the podium via a back door, not a secret platform. He comes out waving, smiling, flashing the V sign and looking natural doing so. He is accompanied by Cosmos public relations man John O'Rielly and his personal interpreter Julio Mazzei. The newspeople applaud.

Pelé wears the kind of clothes that only wealthy professional athletes and/or actors can wear, clothes that make anyone else look like they're waiting to get mugged. He wears a white suit with red pinstripes, a white shirt with a black and red striped tie, white socks (not sweats) and white patent leather shoes. Pelé has an easy, friendly

145

smile, a smile reflecting confidence and encouraging friendship. There is no underlying air of slickness about Pelé and though his eyes match his pinstripes, reflecting the fatigue of promotions, traveling and games, he appears relaxed and congenial.

Steve Leipsner (then general manager of the Diplomats who was made an "advisor" when the club was sold) makes a few comments including the announcement that 26,000 tickets have been sold in advance, thereby assuring record NASL attendance for tomorrow's game. John O'Reilly takes over and explains that Pelé will take questions one-by-one going by seating order.

Although O'Reilly has asked everyone to speak English, several media type who know some Portuguese, Pelé's native language, figure this may be their only chance to use it, so they do to the consternation of the less educated and to interpreter Mazzei, who must translate both the question and Pelé's answer into English. Some of the newsmen don't ask questions at all; instead, they make welcome to America speeches which Pelé graciously accepts. Others hand him souvenirs (a switch, since Pelé is usually the souvenir provider) including a copy of *Soccer America* Magazine featuring him on its cover, and a Brazilian national team jersey. Some questions are asked; even a few good ones:

Papers in Brazil say you will play on Brazil's nation team in the next World Cup. Will you?

"If at that time I am in good shape I will play for them," Pelé finally responds after allowing how he has a pretty long way to go before he's in that kind of shape.

What about the violent crowds in Boston?

"I don't see violence. People treat me nicely all over the world. The only problem is when fans want to take my

146

clothing off." Quick smile, bringing laughter.

Would you work with the U.S. national team as a player or coach?

"If I received an invitation to be coach of the Olympic or World Cup team, it would be a great thing in my life. I would receive such an invitation with great interest." (Is the USSF listening?)

How did you get your nickname?

"When I was little, my friends called me Pelé. I don't know why, and I don't know what it means, but I was lucky because everyone in the world can say it."

Can soccer in the United States reach high international standards and how long will it take?

"Kids in the United States are natural sports people and I see a lot of them playing soccer. For this reason I believe that in a few years soccer in this country will be in a higher positon than other countries on the international level."

What do you think about women and girls playing soccer?

"It is not common in Brazil but it is in Europe. (Pause) It would be difficult for announcers to follow a woman's game though. How would they say a woman trapped the ball with her chest?" (Pelé will not score many goals with women's lib that way.)

Has you busy schedule affected your conditioning or play?

"Sure, I'm a little tired, but my purpose is to help soccer grow in this country, not just score goals."

How has your wife adjusted to your life?

"My wife knew what kind of life I led. (Pelé married Rose in 1966, ten years into his carer.) As you know, the woman is never satisfied because I'm not home," he says teasing the woman who asked the question.

The press conference ends. Newsmen and others who had been granted admittance crowd to the front of the room, seeking autographs. Pelé remains patient. He has not sat down since before the conference began over an hour ago, yet he seems determined to see everyone satisfied. After fifteen minutes of autograph signing, posing for pictures, and making small talk, he goes upstairs to his motel room. Jon Rose breathes a sigh of relief as the reporters file out.

The Pelé news conference, meeting with President Ford, and huge advance ticket sale were the end results of the most hectic week in Washington Diplomat history. When Pelé comes to a town everyone—players, coach, PR men, general manager, club owners—works harder. Temporary secretarial help is brought in to help with ticket requests for the Diplomats game. Tempers run a little shorter, and the normally pleasant Diplomats office is slightly tense.

Thom Meredith, who shares public relatons chores with Jon Rose for the Dips and who, at 23, is a soccer encyclopedia with glasses, was touchy three days before the Pelé visit about a non-Pelé subject. "No one in the league office or at the USSF knows the score of the game last night between the U.S. national team and Poland and it's 10:30 in the morning," he says slamming down the telephone receiver and not accepting the explanation that the game was played in Seattle as a viable excuse. When someone comments on his irritability, he admits it's part of the Pelé pressure (Poland won 4-0 he found out around noon.) The press conference and meeting with the

President have been on-again off-again, the game program (a special Pelé-enlarged edition) is incomplete and security must be double-checked.

For Diplomats coach Dennis Viollet the pressure is most intense. His team is skidding and he must prepare them to play the rejuvenated Cosmos. It will be the Diplomats' first game of the season at R.F.K. and there will be a huge crowd he'd like to impress with a win.

Viollet shares his office and his red, white and blue telephone with Alan Spavin; a 33-year old midfielder from England whom Viollet recently appointed assistant coach. There is no portable movie screen, fancy intercom system or plush carpeting that a head coach in American football might have. Only a couple of pennants, a few boxes of shoes, some practice jerseys in a corner, and assorted papers.

Coach and assistant face each other from behind their desks as they talk. Both are truly soccer men who, combined, total nearly 40 years of professional soccer experience between them. Viollet, angular, an excellent player in his day for Manchester United, and a survivor of the much publicized plane crash in Munich in 1959 which killed many of his teammates. He wears dark glasses indoors and out. Spavin, despite his age one of the top two or three midfielders in the NASL, is rounder, more athletic looking than Viollet. He owns a legitimate betting parlor in England. Both men are capable of being humorous; neither is with Pelé on the way. They talk of how they will prepare the team for him and what he means to the game.

"No matter who you play against in soccer, you can't start worrying too much about one player," Viollet says.

"It's a team game. If you worry about one player too much, it affects everyone on the team.

"We're going to put one man on him—Roy Willner. He's. young and quick and will help cut down Pelé's effectiveness." Willner, 25, is a former junior All-American from Catonsville Junior College in Maryland who was called on to start after injuries knocked out some first team players. He has played well, and the head-to-head confrontation of Young American Willner versus the Old International Superstar-Legend is not without symbolic meaning at least.

Spavin concurs with Viollet's strategy and indicates it won't be too hard to keep from being distracted by Pelé's presence. "Naturally, everyone's excited about playing against Pelé," he says, "but once you're in the game you get so involved, you don't realize what one particular player is doing all the time."

"There's a lot of pressure on Pelé, too," says Viollet. "A lot of people will be seeing him for the first time. Unfortunately so many will expect him to perform the impossible, some may go away disappointed. But not just one person can make that big a difference in soccer."

Of course, Viollet was talking about on the field. At the box office, he admits, it's different.

"Pelé's the only soccer player this country knows about," he says. "They don't know (Franz) Beckenbauer (of West Germany) or (Johann) Cruyff (of 1974 Holland national team fame—or infamy, depending upon which accounts of his performance you prefer.) So they come to see him, but I hope we can get some new fans out of Pelé.

"I'm a little frightened, though, that he'll cause what happened in '67 and '68 to start up again. Other clubs might start bringing in other expensive players. If you start spending, you must be able to afford it. Now most clubs have their heads above water financially. If everyone is buying players, those teams that aren't winning won't have any people going to the games and then they'll be in trouble. We'll be going backwards if we start bringing in players from the outside again."

"It all amounts to a hell of a burden for Pelé," Spavin interjects. "Everyone is expecting so much from him. If he doesn't score a lot of goals, fans will be disappointed."

"Don't forget, Pelé brings out the best in opposing players," says Viollet, sounding perhaps just a little more hopeful than he wanted. "Players like the atmosphere; they like crowds. Sunday should be a good game."

Sunday was not a good game; not for the Dips anyway. Pelé disappointed no one in the league record crowd of 35,620 at R.F.K., as he scored two goals (one a 30 yard blast; the other a three foot chip shot into an unprotected net) and was credited with two assists as he definitely led the Cosmos to a 9-2 rout of the Diplomats.

Viollet's strategy to keep from overplaying Pelé did not work, as Washington was preoccupied with the legend; but then, he forced them to be. After pacing himself for the first 15 minutes, Pelé gradually took control of the game. He was the master of what an old pro should be, expending only as much energy as needed and only when needed. Anytime he was within 20 yards of the goal, he showed what soccer buffs call "finishing skill"— an ability to score or help a teammate score. Or, to Americanize—he smelled the goal; he's a money player. He did it despite physically tough play by Roy Willner who shoved Pelé, cut his legs out from under him, and, in general, marked him tightly. It just didn't matter. When Pele was ready, he did just about whatever he wanted.

Following the game, Willner was in the unusual situation of being surrounded by reporters. Willner, built like a stocky scholastic wrestler with a short, strong neck and sturdy legs, showed genuine nonchalance at the whole atmosphere and an unaware locker room visitor might have initially suspected him of being on the winning team. "I wanted to beat him to the ball, but he's so quick he just beat me," said Willner. "But it was great. I loved it; not the losing, of course, but playing against Pelé.

"He's a real quarterback out there. At the beginning of the game he was telling them (his Cosmos teammates) to slow it down and when they didn't right away, he got angry.

"Then he started to open up. He talked to me a lot out there. He told me to go forward—away from him a litle—and then he'd leave me. He also told me to stop pushing and play soccer, but he gave me a few good stiff arms and an elbow or two. It's just part of the game."

The Cosmos dressing room looked liked an impromptu international party guarded by special police. Not only were press passes checked, but the bearers were fixed with hard stares aimed at shaking down intruders. They were "Are you sure you want to be here?" stares; the kind designed to reduce grizzly newsmen into weakfish who would say, "Gee, I really didn't feel like bothering Pelé anyway; just tell him hello for me, okay, guys?"as they back pedalled out of the muggy room. It didn't work. Pelé was surrounded by newsmen, though a couple of slightly crazed rent-a-cops kept nudging reporters backward. Questions are difficult to ask with a couple of pudgy fingers in your gut, and answers are hard to hear halfway across a noisy locker room. Flanking maneuvers, where some newsmen decoyed the security boys while others asked questions, finally wore the guards down.

Pelé sat half dressed on a stool calm and smiling. One reason he was smiling was because one of the special plainclothesmen was fanning him with a towel. He was calm because he was Pelé. He answered questions, was photographed, and signed autographs while dressing.

"I am not the only savior of American soccer," Pelé said, a comment which may surprise many around the NASL who think he is. "Everyone who plays the game is a savior." He pulled on his blue pants.

"Today, I played on a real soccer field for the first time since I came to the United States and it felt very good. I feel good." He slipped into a blue and white horizontally striped shirt.

"The man who played me forgot this is a team game," he said of Willner. "He played me too closely and that was his mistake." He put on a white leather jacket. An autograph seeker thrust out a pen which made a small ink spot on the jacket. Pelé didn't seem to notice; he signed the paper anyway and a few bodyguards gave some pointed advice to media types, "Let him give the kids some autographs. Give him some air."

Roy Willner poked his head into the Cosmos locker room. He was as unnoticed as Pelé's Cosmos teammates. Seeing Pelé ringed by admirers and some Brazilian-brand Gestapo, Willner turned around to leave. "I had a kid get his autograph for me," he admitted. "I just wanted to tell Pelé thanks." With that, Willner called out, "Thanks, Pelé!" and left.

For the next two games at R.F.K., the Dips averaged slightly over 2,000 people per game.

Yes, Pelé can pack them in and rarely does he disappoint. He has turned many a city in the U.S. and all over the world on its ear with his visits. The NASL sent teams separate attendance figures for games in which Pelé played, and throughut the season he always averaged around the 20,000 mark. For this attention-getting power, Pelé deserves, and gets, high grades.

"Pelé's easily given us his millions back in publicity," says Dennis Viollet.

"Pelé's (tax free) salary averages out to something like $44,000 per game," Greg Myers figures. "I guess the question is, 'Will it be a long term love affair so he'll be worth it?' I personally think it will continue. Pelé is a genius in soccer. He's a gentleman and he's concerned with his image as far as kids go."

"I have to look with hindsight at the signing of Pelé," Lamar Hunt admits. "Now, I'd say it was positive but I really didn't think it would be this successful. I didn't realize he would get as much attention in the U.S. as he has."

"Pelé provides so many intangible, benefits," says Seattle head coach John Best, whose Sounders dumped Pelé and his teammates 2-0 before a national television audiene on July 5, 1975 by playing an alert zone defense. "He's added so much credibility to our league. People overseas used to look down on us, but now the whole world believes in our league.

"Pelé pulls in crowds, which is what teams want. Once the crowd is there it gives.teams the chance to make some new soccer fans."

With all due respect, to Dennis, Greg, Lamar and John, Pelé has given soccer in U.S.A. only an image of big league success, skill and acceptance because he has all those qualities. But the reality of the game itself is far removed from that image. Pelé has upstaged soccer. The vacuum created when he leaves town makes that all too apparent—get rid of the temporary help, no need for extra security, forget about overselling. The Pelé Show is so big it detracts from the regular attraction. No doubt, teams that hosted Pelé and the Cosmos were thankful for the big pay days. But much more significant to the sport as it grows in the U.S. are the enthusiastic capacity crowds that turned out late in the 1975 season to see the Settle Sounders and Portland Timbers compete for first place in the Western Division. Nor was it Pelé who turned the highly Americanized St. Louis Stars into Central Division champions. In the area of critical issues such as Americanization, salaries, professional status and the national team, Pelé's input is largely symbolic—some young American talent may be drawn to soccer with hopes of becoming another Pelé, getting his kind of attention, making his kind of money; but the reality of what pro soccer holds is not found in Pelé.

The Pelé mystique continues, as it must.

Pelé is indeed an unusual person, capable of handling fame and fortune with humility.

Pelé· is admirable for his friendliness toward all specially youth, and his willingness to assist teammates and others with developing soccer skills.

Pelé is still a great soccer player in the manner of an old pro who knows what to do and when and how to do it.

Pelé would make an excellent choice a s an assistant national team coach (providing of course, the USSF ever appoints a fulltime head coach) to teach fundamentals.

Pelé would make an excellent floating exhibition player, hired by the NASL to go around and play with different NASL teams against other NASL teams each week in games labelled strictly as exhibitions. This would keep Pele in the proper perspective—a goodwill ambassador for American soccer distinguishable from the real games and season.

However, the Pele of 1975 does not fit in American soccer, and deep down the throngs that sold out stadiums to see him must know it. They went to see a living legend, the great Pele Show, not two teams in a North American Soccer League game. From out in the heartland, on the campus of Penn St. University, a huge college community in the middle of rural America, comes the indignant voice of Walter Bahr:

"They paid Pele $7 million? I'd rather see the Annandale (Va.) Boys Club against a Philadelphia Boys Club. They're making a circus out of the professional game now."

Pelé in a familiar pose — flashing the triumphant "V" sign and looking natural doing so. *Photo by John E. de Freitas.*

7. The Reality: Kyle Rote, Jr.

There is no better example of the area soccer must capture in order to survive than that around the metroplex of Dallas, Texas. Flat, neat, green, old yet accepting new growth with a downhome grin and a clap on the shoulder, there's a sense of pride and friendliness reserved for something or someone local making good. To outsiders, or the skeptical, or the cynical, the fondness seems overbearing at times, and when the Texan leaves his home to visit up north or east, he may hear the slurs, "Hick" or "Grit" and they pain him just as millions of Americans were pained to here President Lyndon Johnson say, "Nigra" time and again. And, of course, there's the sepcial stigma attached to the events of November 22, 1963, especially when a visitor drives in the area and what were just sad radio or TV broadcasts become reality in the form or roads, buildings, and places: "The Preisdent and Mrs. Kennedy had arrived at Love Airport . . ." "The President has been taken to Parkland Hospital . . ."

But these are new times with a generation of young people growing up who will only read of Johnson and Kennedy. They are the today and tomorrow of the area, and they will provide the people there with history and legends of their own, enriched, no doubt, by a phenomenon John Steinbeck noted in *Travels with Charley*; "Texas has its own private history based on, but not limited by, facts."

Soccer needs a piece of that kind of history, the history that spreads and grows by word of mouth. When Texans swap stories at their barbeques about the local high school's new goalkeeper or argue about the trade between the Tornado and the Thunder, then socer will know it has a place in Americana.

Highland Park High School in Dallas is situated on a neatly etched plot of green in the middle of established suburbia. Near the school are carefully primped homes belonging to the wealthy and materially secure. Highland Park High has kept the neighborhood happily chatting for years about its local boys who have made the big time including football's Doak Walker and the free-spirited Bobby Layne.

In 1973, Kyle Rote Jr., the standout of Highland Park High's football, basketball and baseball teams four years earlier, signed a professional soccer contract for a $1400 salary to play with the Dallas Tornado. That wasn't exactly what was expected of such a bright high school prospect, especially one who was the namesake of another great local football player who played his college ball at Southern Methodist University in Dallas. But senior was a good ol' boy and junior was too, so the locals figured "Fine; let's see what he can do."

All Kyle Jr. did was win Rookie of the Year and the NASL scoring title in 1973, the first time for an American in either category, and then in the winter of 1974, he flat out whipped the likes of O.J. Simpson, Franco Harris and other major sports biggies in the ABC-TV sponsored

158

Superstars competition. Junior showed how to do things Texas style, and he's been celebrity status ever since.

But soccer, despite its need for fan identification with American performers, has been neither able, nor altogether willing, to fully promote its one American supername. The dilemma is as follows: the NASL needs American players with ability and charisma; Rote has both but the latter is well-developed while the former is still developing. Adding to the dilemma is the fact that Rote is not afraid to talk about and act upon changes he feels will improve the game and help it gain acceptance in the U.S.

Kyle Rote Jr. knows the realities of American pro soccer. Using an interesting blend of fair play befitting the ministry student he once was, and calculation, befitting the law student he once was, Rote is attempting to upgrade the game for players in reality as well as in image. Despite All-American looks (blonde hair, blue-eyes, turned-up nose, six-foot, 190 pounds), background (a tuition paying honor student at the University of the South after leaving a football scholarship at Oklahoma St. because he was disatisfied with his grades), and life style (churchgoer, non-smoker, non-curser, strictly social drinker, married to Lynne, who is also blonde), there's more than a little radical in Rote, especially for an American soccer player since they are supposed to sit tight, learn, and play for pocket change if at all.

In Dallas recognition of Rote ranges from husband-to-wife whispers like, "Hey, that's Kyle Rote Jr." to slaps on the back by leathery men saying things like, "Kyle, I been watchin' yew since yew was in hah school." The Rotes are fiendly, sincere blue jeans, T-shirt and sneakers people. Their modest rambler in suburban Dallas is informal, decorated with a threadbare sofa, a stereo on crates, an appealingly disorganized office, three adopted cats, and a handwritten sign on the front door requesting, "Please knock, bell out of order." The Rotes don't try to fool others about their position in life, and they don't try to fool themselves.

After winning approximately $54,000 in the 1974 Superstars contest, Rote gave $20,000 to assorted charities. "Of course, it helps with taxes," he says honestly, "but there's no sense getting used to a life style you can't maintain."

Rote's natural athletic ability was not the only reason he won the Superstars competition. In fact, he says he feels he got in as a member of one of the "weird" sports. "After I won Rookie of the Year and the scoring title, I got a couple of endorsements and my Dad advised me to get an agent," Rote remembers. "So I joined the Mark McCormack agency (McCormack is one of the country's leading agents for sports figures) and he called me one day and asked if I'd be interested in the Superstars. He said Roone Arledge (ABC-TV's sports director) wanted more varied competition. I guess the Superstars people figured a soccer player would provide filler for the name athletes from the other sports.

"So I started preparing myself, I crammed a notebook with notes from 56 different reference books. I figured I'd better be prepared because it was a one shot deal—if you don't do well, they don't invite you back. I had to be sure that if I finished 48th out of 48, I'd still be able to say I gave my best mentally and physically.

"I was in seminary school at the time, so it was a tight schedule. I worked out early in the evenings and took a one a.m. run every day."

Kyle Rote Jr. goes high in the air over John Sewell, player and coach of the highly Americanized St. Louis Stars. *Dallas Tornado photo.*

Rote shows he can outreach an opponent when he has to through a little additional determination. *Photo by Raff Franco.*

Though he was only 23 at the time, Rote's preparation combined with a lifetime of familiarity with big names in sports kept him from being awed by his competition. "I have a great deal of respect for guys like (John) Havlicek, (Franco) Harris and (Rod) Laver,"Rote says. "But I've known so many pros, I know they're human just like anyone else. They're not single-faceted people. They feel the same pressures, or more, than others. Deep down, though, I honestly didn't think I had much of a chance.

"I didn't treat any of them as a fan would. Even though I might have wanted an autograph, I didn't ask for it."

Taking that kind of attitude into the Superstars is just one hint of Rote's tough side. Just because he happens to enjoy people and prefers to treat them politely doesn't mean he's a gawking, wide-eyed, young straight arrow from a not quite major sport, who can't handle the big boys in competition or in the front office. The Superstars proved to a lot of people that Junior was no easy mark.

Rote won first place in tennis, swimming and bowling, took second in golf and bicycling, and finished out of the money in baseball hitting and the half mile. "It was a relief when it was over," he says. "I was thankful for the chance to compete and for the chance to develop my potential. I was happy to represent soccer which was considered a second class sport played by second class athletes.

"I was most thankful for a wife willing to do two loads of sweaty laundry each day for me."

While Rote wasn't naive enough to think that the attention he brought himself and soccer by winning the

Superstars in 1974 and finishing third in 1975 automatically raised the game to major sport status, he knew it increased his worth to the Tornado and soccer. Rote appears on posters with the likes of such household faces as Billie Jean King and Larry Csonka. He has a weekly radio show, assorted endorsements, does sports commentary on nationwide television, and travels across the country talking soccer, sports in general, and the good clean living he believes in.

He doesn't say yes to everything. "There were a lot of get rich quick schemes from the start," Rote says. "One old guy had developed a soccer helmet he wanted me to endorse. A few people call and just ask for money. I try to explain that I give to certain charities that would more than likely help them. I even give them phone numbers to call. It's sad."

And not everything brings direct financial gain. Some speeches, camps and posters, he admits doing "for the good of the game." He adds that he was perhaps a little too generous with his time after the Superstars victory to the point where it hindered his onfield performance. "Because of Superstars," Rote says in retrospect, "whatever I could get into to promote soccer, I'd say, 'Let's do it.' But it affected my play in 1974, so I've had to be more careful."

One of the activities Rote has not given up is running the Kyle Rote Jr. Superstar Soccer Camp located in Sandy Lake Park near Dallas. He visits the park several times weeks before the soccer camp opens in late June in order to make sure the facilities meet his approval. Prior to leaving his house Lynne gives him the names of some children to remember when he gets to camp and he repeats them a couple of times. He asks if she needs anything from the store, she says no, he gives her a Texas-sized squeeze and leaves.

He drives about semi-fast in a fairly new, moderately cluttered Mustang fastback, while half listening to a rock music station several decibals away from blaring, and engaging part-time in his one prominent vice—nibbling, not biting, his fingernails, not at the tips, as is traditional, but in the middle so the palm is turned away from the face. Outside, as the flatland goes by, evidence of the great Texas cola war proliferates as signs of the veteran favorite Dr. Pepper (pronounced "Paper" in Texas) try to look more enticing than brash newcomer Mr. Pibbs (pronounced "Pebbs").

"Bob Lilly and Walt Garrison (of football's Cowboys) had camps here, but they didn't work out," Rote says as he parks the car. "We had pretty good luck last summer (1974) though. I make sure I'm at the camp every day. I don't believe in just lending my name to things. It's not good in a business sense, for one thing—one bad venture and you're through. But it's not fair to the kids either; they expect me to be here."

Rote, his wife, and several trained camp staffers run the camp over two five day sessions which go from 9:00 a.m. to 4:00 p.m. daily. For $43.50 per session almost 200 boys and girls per week swim, golf, ride amusement park rides, learn some soccer, get a daily lunch, a camp T-shirt and a Superstar Barbeque Banquet with their parents and Rote at the end of the week. And Rote just loves every second of it, right? Not exactly.

"The kids are fun," he says, "but they would drive me nuts if I had them for the whole summer. Lynne and I are always worrying about accidents and drownings, even though our staffers are fully trained—it's a big respon-

164

sibility. We're exhausted by the end of each day. But after I retire from soccer, we'd like to run a camp for exceptional children and this is giving us some background in it."

As Rote walks around the sprawling, informal, somewhat disorganized park to check out the area where his camp will be held, he is at his outgoing best. The owner of the camp is a grizzled and gray older man named Frank Rush, who looks and acts very Texas in jeans, putting his arm around the shoulders of some visitors and barking at a small group of kids who are acting rowdy. He hands Rote a Dr. Pepper (score one for the veteran) while the two talk camp business. When a group of girls giddily recognizes Rote; Rush says to an observer, "See that! People like this boy."

A middle-aged woman watching a band festival which is going on in a huge tent near the rides spots Rote and asks, "Isn't that Kyle Rote Jr?" Told that it is indeed, she excitedly tells her friends and they all send their children over for autographs. Rote happily signs, bending over to say to the children, "Hi! How're yew?" A boy of about twelve watching the activity, waits until the other children leave before coming up to Rote and asking not for an autograph, but for money. A little perplexed, Rote frowns slightly but puts a nickel into the boy's hand.

Rote remembers the names Lynne had told him so he greets two of Rush's grandchildren by name. Rush looks pleased as Rote leaves the park.

Rote does not act superior and people seem to sense it (perhaps he *should* act superior to help ward off twelve year old panhandlers). Convinced that he can serve others and himself well, Rote is succeeding. But Rote has to serve the game he plays well, too. And success there has

165

been more difficult to achieve. The truth is that without the money and subsequent endorsements from Superstars, Rote would be just another soccer moonlighter. At dinner over lasagna and chianti, at home watching a rerun of one of his favorite movies, *The Good the Bad and the Ugly,* while Lynne weaves the early stages of a rug, or whenever he is engaged in conversation about the state of American soccer, Rote exhibits the kind of thinking that may yet make the sport truly professional.

To begin with, though Rote's current contract prohibits him from specifying his salary to the public or his teammates, he says that those who believe he is the NASL's second highest paid player are wrong.

"I suppose the general consensus among the public and players is that I'm the highest paid (behind Pelé), but I'm not," Rote says. "Reports that I signed a three-year (1974-76) contract for $25,000 per year are way off. Even a total of $25,000 over three years is off. But the owners don't like players communicating about things like contracts and they've been preventing it since 1967."

But Rote's complaint is not with his own salary as much as it is with the whole salary structure in the NASL, which is just one of the reasons he's pushing for a Soccer Players Association.

"When I started to get involved in forming an association, I was doing some public relations type work for the Tornado," Rote says. "But I didn't think it would be a good idea to be on the club payroll if I was going to be active in the formation of the association, so I gave up the job."

Rote knows an association is likely to be viewed dimly by loan players and management alike, but, he says, "Soccer will have to take care of American players with money eventually. Lamar Hunt could pay us $9,000 or $12,000 but he doesn't want to set a precedent with loan players available for less."

Lynne Rote elaborates on other difficulties caused by the low salaries: "There's not much social life with a soccer team and soccer players don't make enough money to keep up with athletes in other sports. But the worst part is that people won't really see soccer players as professionals as long as the players also must work at some other occupation as well."

In their drive to upgrade the professionalism in soccer, the Rotes have done a complete contract analysis and sent their comments and recommendations to labor lawyers. When the S.P.A. becomes a reality, their work will no doubt be reflected in newly proposed contracts. Insurance, or rather the lack of it, is one area of the current contract that specifically disturbs the Rotes, an area they consider more immediately pressing than salary.

"In Dallas, we really have no insurance provisions," Kyle says. "Our contract says that if we're injured in the scope of employment the club will pay us our salaries. We're really assuming the risk of playing on our own.

"I suppose that the club would feel a moral obligation pay for a player injured during a game. But really, our contract doesn't define 'scope of employment'.

"Does it include driving to and from games and practices? Does it include preseason and off-season conditioning?"

For now, Rote and other players are covered through private policies which generally cost more than group plans.

The appearance of Pelé on the NASL scene will

"make all non commital players anxious to see a players association formed," Rote believes. The reason? "It's unprecedented in sports where you have a player making twice the combined total of every other player in the league."

Rote seems to be good at math:

The total three year Pelé package amounted to a little over $7 million, about $2.4 million per year. Taking $60,000 as the salary ceiling (a figure Rote really believes to be about $4,000 too high) for each of the 20 NASL teams, the total salary bqdget for the NASL is $1.2 million. $2.4 million for Pele is twice the $1.2 million for the rest of the 360 or so players in the league.

"The attack isn't on Pelé," says Rote, not backing off the issue, but attempting to keep it in proper focus, "because he'll earn his money by promoting the game. The attack is on the discrepency between what we've (NASL players) been told in the past; that as teams could afford it, we'd get more money.

"If the money that teams are paying to help pay Pelé's contract were taken and spread around, it would raise salaries, not by much but it would help. The reason Pelé draws so well is half him and half the result of youth clinics that players around the league have been working so hard at for years."

That may not be the kind of talk that will make Rote a sweetheart to management, but it's honest talk, and though it is delivered businesslike, it's a little proud; a little emotional. Rote is not anti-Pelé; rather, he is hoping professional soccer leaders in America will remember those players who have been living in soccer's demanding but uncertain real world. Rote, because of his Superstars fame and because of "a family name which relates to two generation of sports that has helped me immeasurably," has risen to prominence as a representative of the world of U.S. soccer. But he knows that for others to do the same and for the U.S to become a respected professional world soccer power, the sport must change. Deep down, he has real hope that it will.

"When I first started playing soccer at 17 there were no more than a hundred soccer players around Dallas (there are now over 40,000)," he recalls, "and I was selected for the southwest United States all-star team. We travelled to England to play, and I really saw our limited view of sports in the United States. Ten times the number of people watch the World Cup than watch the Super Bowl.

"We really don't understand how big soccer is beyond our borders. It's a political event. It's Israel being banned from the Asian soccer games. It's Brezhnev watching the Soviet soccer team on TV while Nixon went to a Russian ballet. We can't forget our own U.S. sports, but we must have a world view too.

"Soccer games in the U.S. are played off-the-cuff right now. But eventually it will evolve into a more sophisticated game, more complex operations, more mental demands. Really, we haven't transformed the general soccer interest and feeling in this country to pro soccer yet.

"Really, the fact that owners seem to be in the game for business, not prestige, is good because they want to protect their investments and make them grow. They're not in it for prestige, because it's not a glamour sport yet, like football is. So the future of pro soccer is good; we're catching it on the upswing.

"With 250 million players in the world, the playing

possibilities are limitless. I'm certain that some day there will be a Dallas-Moscow rivalry in soccer just as today there's a Dallas-St. Louis rivalry."

So Rote's goals are not altogether different than Phil Woosnam's or Lamar Hunt's or anyone else who wants to see American soccer grow strong. It's his means that contrast with the organization line, a sometimes dangerous position career-wise for an athlete to take. Making things extra precarious for Rote is his admission that "the amount of attention I get is not equal to my ability. I'm not as valuable a player to the team as, for example, Roy Turner, but I get more publicity than him."

"Naturally there's some resentment," Rote knows, "but my teammates have really been patient and unbelievably understanding, all things considered. In Los Angeles last year I stepped off the plane and I was immediately hustled off to a radio show. I missed part of the practice and the time I missed with the other players was valuable to developing rapport on the road."

Rote's 1974 performance fell to seven goals and two assists, down from the ten and ten of 1973, but still a good season by most standards. His time away from the team, improvement in the level of competition caused by better foreign players, and the added attention he was getting from defenders combined to cause the slump. At the start of the 1975 season, he seemed back in good form, but Tornado coach Ron Newman did not seem pleased with Rote's performance in the season's first three games (the Tornado lost two of them), though Rote scored a goal and had two assists. So when Washington came to town in early May, Newman benched Rote for the entire game, to the chagrin of the Dallas front office which knows Rote's charisma, and the Dallas fans who like to see those home

As a "target" man, Rote is expected to score on set-ups in front of the opponents' goal and go up for the ball in a crowd. *Photo by Raff Franco.*

You can't always use your head as here Rote concentrates on kicking a pass downfield. *Photo by Steve Hammond.*

town boys playing. Rote spent much of the game nail nibbling on the end of the Dallas bench looking just a bit self-conscious as a group of kids began a "We want Rote!" cheer. It didn't work, and neither did leaving Rote on the bench. Dallas lost 2-0.

After the game, Newman was in a corner of the locker room speaking quietly but animatedly with a couple of players about the loss, while other members of the Tornado sat quietly and dressed slowly. Rote, still in full uniform, was in an opposite corner of the locker room kicking a soccer ball hard against the wall, offering kicks to a ball boy nearby.

"He (Newman) didn't say anthing about not playing to me," Rote said.

"Kyle didn't play because I felt we needed an extra defender opposite Randy Horton," was Newman's postgame explanation.

"It was a decision Ron and I will have to sit down and talk about tomorrow" said Tornado general manager Bob Power who was evidently not pleased with the benching particularly in light of the loss. "Of course, it was Ron's decision, but there's the variable of fan appeal to be considered too."

By the next evening things hadn't changed much, although Newman and Rote were in the mood to make some carefully worded comments about one another while Power was simply saying, "I'm not an expert on talent, but I think Rote is a good soccer talent and I would have played him."

Newman alluded to contrary feelings:

"Kyle has the potential to be a good player if he's with a good team, but on a struggling team he's not that helpful. I had to take someone out of the line, and Kyle

172

was the only one not playing up to par. It would have been an insult to have taken out one of the other players and left Kyle in.

"No one has put any pressure on me to use Kyle. I just explained that right now I can't afford to play him. If I ever was pressured by management to play Kyle, I'd just say, 'If you'll take the responsibility if we lose, I'll play him.'

"Kyle works hard and he's a good air player. But he must score or assist to help the team. Lately, he's not playing that well."

Rote, who was Dallas' fourth leading all-time scorer as he entered the 1975 season, his third in the NASL, had a somewhat different point of view of his benching and the game against the Diplomats:

"I expected to start. Last week after we beat Denver 5-0 Ron said this was his best team ever, so I didn't expect any change.

"It's a case of respect for one another as individuals. I respect his authority as coach, but I disagree with his decision. I at least thought he should respect me enough to have some communication with me before the game to tell me his reasons.

"There are teams in this league, like Washington, that have a coaching influence and there are teams like us, where players are expected to play on their own. They had a strategy against us, while we had no attacking strategy.

"We had eleven individuals playing out there. That style of play—a non-coaching style—requires that our players really get to know one another on the field. You can't always get that chemistry this early in the season.

"Sitting on the bench is nothing you can enjoy. You

173

can't do more than your best, so you just have to keep working hard."

By mid-season Rote was leading the Tornado in scoring. Immediately following the 1975 season, Newman was fired as coach of the Tornado.

Still, opinions on Rote's soccer playing ability are never very glowing, yet observers invariably wind up saying, "but he does seem to score goals." There have been worse things said about American soccer players.

John Best, coach of the Seattle Sounders, was an assistant to Ron Newman in Dallas when Rote broke into pro soccer. Of Rote as a soccer player Best says, "It's a miracle he could start so late in life (17) and do so well in the pros. He's a heck of an athlete and he has a knack of seeing through to the root of something and working on it.

"He's a good target man to set up for a score because he's good with his head and with balls in the air. Even when he first came up he scored when there was just a ghost of a chance. We didn't want him to become a wizard dribbling the ball. But as his team has changed, more things are becoming required of him in different skills areas, so he'll have to work at them."

Al Collins, coach and general manager of the Baltimore Comets, feels, "Rote is on the same level as a player as most Americans in this league."

John Sewell who, as coach of the St. Louis Stars, is very aware of American talent says, "Rote makes himself useful on the field."

So goes the soccer playing litany of Kyle Rote. It relfects what everyone around the league knows—that American talent needs coaching and developing; and it takes time to do that. It sometimes means playing someone for better or for worse, but gambling on players who are aggressive, willing and able to learn makes sense for soccer's development in the U.S.A. Rote just happens to be the best known of such players and because of his fame he's able to cope with, though not altogether accept, his situation.

"Lynne's family and mine still ask me when I'm going to work for a living," Rote says with a grin.

Rote can afford to work at soccer, or at least at keeping in shape for soccer, while other players are on their fulltime jobs. Keeping in condition *is* part of Rote's fulltime job, so he gets in his mile-and-a-half of running and maybe a light workout at the Institute of Aerobic Research in Dallas, the dream fitness facility offering swimming, an indoor track, an outdoor jogging course that winds around ponds, trees and ducks, tennis, racquet ball and more. He studies personal notes of his games and works at correcting weak points and further refining already sharp ones.

The athlete in Rote emerged naturally since he was not pushed by his famous father, a member of pro football's Hall of Fame. "My father was a big influence on me, but I don't think he wanted to be," says Rote. "I had to practically beg him just to play catch with me. He convinced me you need something to fall back on. He indicated to me that he'd be just as happy if I were a musician or teacher. There was no pressure to be a professional athlete."

But Kyle was drawn to sports. His success in high school sports, which did not include soccer, led to scholarship offers from 50 colleges. By the time he graduated from the University of the South, in Sewanee, Tenn., he received offers to tryout as a quarterback for the

New York Giants (his father's old team), Atlanta Falcons and Dallas Cowboys of the NFL, though he had not played football since his freshman year in college. He chose to play soccer, which he had played for three years at Sewanee, for the Tornado out of pragmatism and a belief that soccer was a growing sport with an unlimited future.

Rote wants to be a part of developing that future both on and off the field. His athletic ability helps him meet the onfield challenges, his grasp of professionalism helps him meet the issues, and his name and nature allow him to help the game. If he must play harder than everyone else to keep off the bench, he will. If he must be the voice of change to upgrade the working conditions and benefits of soccer players in the U.S., he will be. If he can help promote the game to the public, he's willing.

Late in the 1975 season the Dallas Tornado flew into Baltimore for a game against the Comets. Neither team had much of a season left as the Tornado had only a slim mathematical chance of making the playoffs while Baltimore's chances were even slimmer. Though Rote had played every game since his benching in May, it had not been a rewarding season. Dallas was well on its way to finishing out of the playoffs for the first time since 1970.

Rote was informed in the hotel lobby that two local sportscasters wanted to film him at Towson St. College at 11:00 a.m., a time which conflicted with a team practice Newman had scheduled at Towson Jr. High School across the street from the team's motel. Rote refused to miss practice for TV so Debbie Goldstein, Comets PR director, asked the sportscasters to meet with Rote at the practice site.

After the practice, while his teammates crossed the

street to their motel to shower, eat lunch and relax until game time, Rote, hot and sweaty from the workout in 90 degree heat, patiently talked with Jack Dawson of WMAR-TV sports in his friendly Texan manner, calling Dawson Jack throughout the filming. Andrea Kirby, a spunky feature oriented newswoman from WJZ-TV, first asked Rote basically the same questions Dawson had asked and then had him teach her how to dribble for the camera. Rote complimented Ms. Kirby, whom he called Andrea, as she practiced. Then Rote did a little loosening up routine, bouncing the ball off his foot, knee, shoulder and head at her request.

TV taken care of, Rote spent another five minutes or so tape recording an interview with a journalism student interning with the Comets management staff. He then spent ten minutes talking with and signing autographs for a group of 25 kids who had materialized at the sight of television cameras. A girl of about fourteen offered Rote a small cup of water which he gratefully accepted to her obvious pleasure. At the motel Rote returned a phone call that had come while he was out, showered, was paged in the lobby for another phone call which took another ten minutes, and then he went to the team luch room where the last of his Tornado teammates were finishing their lunches.

"It's like that for Kyle everywhere we go," says Norm Hitzges, the Tornado PR director.

A gathering of less than 3,000 watched the Comets win 3-0 and saw Rote replaced in the second half. There's little arguing that had Pelé been in town, the Comets would have had a sellout. Rote is not the massive draw that Pelé is, but for the American youngster thinking about playing pro soccer in the U.S. someday, or for

177

someone trying to get a more honest look at the state of the game in the States, Rote is a more realistic model. It may be a somewhat discouraging sight, especially for young men thinking of turning pro after college, to see someone who gets as much publicity and works as hard as Rote struggle to stay in the line-up for a mostly foreign team while he also attempts to improve the professional status of players, but it's an honest world they will have to face if they choose to go into pro soccer.

Critics of Rote around the NASL take pleasure in theorizing that if Rote did not have a famous father, he would not be getting the attention or playing time he now gets. And that is the saddest commentary yet, for it is an admission that on soccer's pro level in the U.S. there is little opportunity for recognition, game experience or status as an athlete for the American working his hardest to break into the game on his own. Because of the NASL's predominantly foreign make up and its reluctance to require that four or five Americans actually play at all times during every game, there would not be one nationally known American soccer player without Kyle Rote Jr. And that, no matter how great and progressive an image the NASL tries to convey, is not progress.

For Dallas on the field and at the gate, 1975 was a poor year. Lamar Hunt and Ron Newman both say the low attendance (about 6,000 average not including a 27,000 turnout for an exhibition against Pelé and friends) shows that Rote is more of a draw nationally than in Dallas. "Certainly Kyle is an asset," Hunt adds, "but he's done more around the country than here. Our number one problem as far as attendance goes has been our failure to win games" Hunt also admits that general Tornado promotions "were down this year because we wanted to see what we could draw on our own. We're going to have to pick them up again next year."

Rote feels the attendance problem goes a little further:

"The team has stopped paying attention to the community lately, especially to the kids. In the past we had good rapport with the kids in the area, but now it's deteriorated. It should be picked up again and it should be done for free again. I think most of the players would give their time if the opportunities were there."

Rote sees the development of future fans coming from the handshakes, the greetings like "Hi! How're yew?", the tolerance involved in politely answering innocuous question after innocuous question, the clowning with the media, and the autograph signing in the hot sun or at the busiest of times.

Rote wants the establishment of the true professional soccer player in America by being demanding but equitable on critical issues involving players.

Rote knows the ultimate test of credibility and acceptance will come from the chance for willing and able Americans to perform on the soccer field.

Rote cannot match Pelé in gate appeal, salary, talent or symbolism.

Pelé symbolizes what soccer in the U.S.A. would like to offer its players and fans.

Kyle Rote Jr. symbolizes what it does offer.

Playing the ball in the air is considered Rote's strongest point as a soccer player. *Photo by Raff Franco.*

Kids Get Their Kicks

Phil Woosnam accurately refers to the men playing soccer today as pioneers or missionaries. Their legacy is found in the rapidly growing numbers of children playing soccer today. Soccer played by the young is no longer limited to ethnic groups boxed into small sections of cities and towns. It has worked its way up the feet and into the hearts of young people in all parts of the U.S.A. Soccer has hit suburbia's children in the past three to five years, and for the pro leagues those kids represent soccer's most encouraging sign.

"People are starting to enjoy the enormous appeal of this game," says Greg Myers of Miami who, along with his players has undertaken a community relations project that has put members of the Toros in direct contact with some 150,000 people. "They know now that soccer is not a game dominated by one or two people. In other sports the number of people who actually are in charge with the ball is limited. In baseball, it's primarily the pitcher and catcher. In football, it's the quarterback.

"In soccer, everyone has the chance to be a leader. Everytime a kid gets the ball at his feet, he's in charge. So soccer combines individual appeal with team appeal."

Despite the attractions Myers talks about, despite

soccer's growth on the youth level in Miami at a rate so rapid that, according to Myers, "there aren't enough fields, referees or coaches" to satisfy all who want to participate, game attendance at the pro level in Miami, and many other cities, is still lagging.

Why?

"Soccer is still four to five years away from having really loyal spectators," Myers says as he begins to explain a popular theory around the NASL. "Right now the largest number of participants is in the eight to thirteen year old age group and they must still ask their parents if they want to go to see professional games. When these kids get older, they'll be able to attend games on their own and we'll have larger, more loyal crowds."

Soccer supporters around the country hope that Myers is correct, and leading the hopeful are people with time and money invested in the professional game. If you talk to enough of them about soccer's long range changes of survival, they always wind up saying that the kids hold the key. An interesting grand plan proliferates among the soccer backers in the U.S.A., a plan that shows signs of working. A little fanfare, please, as soccer's popularity progression theory is revealed.

Soccer's Popularity Progression Theory:

Step 1: A lot of young parents who are currently football, baseball, basketball and/or hockey oriented have young children (seven to twelve years old) playing soccer in youth leagues. This at least makes parents cognizant of the game; it even intrigues some who can't see the difficulty in kicking a ball into a net until they try.

Step 2: After a year or two of the kids playing and enjoying the game, the parents take a more active interest. They begin buying their children soccer balls, T-shirts, and tickets to local games—high school, college or pro. At this point, the child's interest stems from his participation in the sport while the parents are becoming more interested in the spectator side by watching the higher quality play at higher levels. The parents' hearts, however, still belong elsewhere, but soccer is moving from being child's play to becoming a sport worth watching.

Step 3: As the youngsters grow into their mid and late teen years, they take their affection for the sport to high school with thm. There it gains acceptance as either a club' or varsity sport and individual players receive attention within the school and eventually in the community. Spectators during this stage are primarily limited to other teenagers, and parents and close friends of the players.

Step 4: When high school soccer programs have had time to develop rivalries with other schools, the spectator appeal becomes broader. The community, which now has a new group of seven to twelve year olds playing the game, begins to respond to the rivalries by attending the high school games. Outstanding high school players become more widely noticed, recognized and accepted by young and old alike. The teenage players and fans begin getting their own drivers licenses at this point, and they begin going to college and pro games on their own.

Step 5: The high school soccer enthusiasts who graduate go to college wanting the opportunity to play and/or watch the sport. Soccer scholarships materialize. At the college level the soccer following is limited in much the same way as it was in Step 3, but with a heavier emphasis on peers.

Step 6: Much the same as Step 4 except collegiate honors, in the form of scholarships or All-American nominations, are more prestigious and receive attention on a wider scale. In the meantime, the second group of seven to twelve year olds is now in high school while another group of seven to twelve year olds is developing an attraction for soccer.

Step 7: A select group of college graduates wish to try and play professionally. They take ten to fifteen years of skill into the game, improving its quality. The improved quality is appreciated by the graduates' parents' generation, which has now had the opportunity to see the young pro's development from childhood through professional status, so the older folks' interest becomes more direct. They do not give up their old favorites in the sports world, but they have developed a genuine interest in, and appreciation for, soccer. The new pros are also followed closely by their peer group, who have been fans all along.

Step 8: As each new group of soccer players progresses through the first seven steps, the game becomes higher in quality and stronger in fan support.

The popularity progression is working. It's not working with the smooth precision that it promises in outline form, but it's working. The particular stage in the progression varies greatly from community to community, but at least today there is a stage in places where five to ten years ago there was a void. St. Louis, for example has completed all eight steps in the progression as the skilled 1975 Stars indicated, whereas places like Pascagoula, Alabama, where there were over 300 registered players in 1974 as compared to only 75 in 1971, are in their first stage. Obviously, St. Louis will mature as a major soccer market before Pascogoula, but within another few years kids in that Alabama town will know and care about who some of the St. Louis Stars players are. According to the

USSF, approximately 600.000 boys and girls play soccer in the U.S.A., although some reports put the figure at one and a half million. In any case, you don't have to look far in most communities to see youth soccer programs either being planned or in full kick.

In suburban Northern Virginia and Maryland, just minutes away from the District of Columbia, soccer has become a family affair on spring and fall weekends. Nearly 60,000 youngsters ranging in age from six on up compete every Saturday and Sunday. Many of them have parents who play in over-30 leagues or in the regularly scheduled pick-up games which have proliferated in recent years. They all share one common bit of enjoyment—they just love kicking the ball hard, long and accurate. It's a new sensation for all of them, one they find challenging and uninhibiting. Since it's just as new to the parents as the kids, dads and moms find it enjoyable to erase America's traditionally negative image of using the kick in sports—as in booting a baseball (for an error), kicking a loose basketball (resulting in a turnover), or having to "settle" for a field goal attempt in football. In soccer you can kick and kick and kick again.

In areas like the D.C. suburbs, where the youth leagues have been established for several years, teams are showing more technique each year, which is both good and bad. On the positive side, improved technique indicates better understanding of the game and closer attention to skills which should improve the overall quality of the game as the players get older. However, the negative side is that too much attention to detail at too early an age is a sure step toward desire-destruction—like fathers who try to teach their ten year olds how to hit a baseball to the opposite field and wind up ruining their ability to hit at all and, consequently, their desire for the game.

Fortunately, youth soccer is still in its formative years in many places so desire-destruction has not yet affected large numbers of kids. In fact, youth soccer leaders in general have shown good sense in working with the young by establishing an everybody plays rule. Not that the rule has been a cure-all. As in all sports, at all levels, disappointment is inescapable and somewhere along the line the majority of people conclude that they wer meant to pursue non-athletic careers. But at least by insuring everyone a chance to play, soccer is not forcing twelve year olds to pack up their hopes.

Pro soccer's survival is tied very closely to the popularity progression, particularly to the uninhibited kicks taken by six, seven, and eight year olds around the U.S. Soccer to the very young is just what it's supposed to be—a game played, not for money and prestige, but for fun. When the littlest of the little get together to play their league games, they don't care about the color of their jersey or if the stripes on their socks match their uniform or what kind of shoes they have on. The game quickly evolves into a formless mass of fun. Coaches scream from the sidelines for positions to be maintained and for players to work the ball, but their pleas go unheard. To the child, soccer means kick and that's what he does. Play sometimes looks like a rugby scrum with every child surrounding the ball and kicking at it. More often it looks like the all-time schoolyard favorite—keep-away, only using feet instead of hands.

The goalkeeper is the most fun to watch. As his teammates race around kicking the ball, he must wait for the infrequent times when the ball escapes the rabble and

186

Goalkeepers have to stop shots any way they can: Above, Ken Cooper of Dallas punches one away. Below, Ian McKechnic, formerly of Boston, leaps high to catch one. *Photos by Steve Hammond.*

someone opens his eyes long enough to see it and breaks for the goal. A seven year old soccer goalie's wait is one of history's most tedious, so it's not unusual for him to swat flies, hum songs, look at airplanes, or wave to his friends during a game. Assuming his attention is diverted to the field soon enough to see a breakaway, which in a game between very young teams looks like a swarm of bees chasing someone who has disturbed their nest, he has to summon up a good deal of courage not to panic at the sight of the stampede. More often than not, the breakaway never reaches the goal; the goalie tires of waiting for action in the net and runs out to join his teammates in the fun part—kicking the ball.

That's the kind of early age play that leads to lasting enjoyment. If the desire is there, slowly instructing technique in later years will be better received. Areas of the country that have moved on to Step 3 or higher in popularity progression are already showing impressive results in the development of skills. Annandale, Va. has one of the country's best developed soccer youth programs after several years of existence. In the fall of 1974 one of its teams in the twelve and thirteen year old age bracket, the Annandale Boys Club Red Wings, travelled to the Netherlands to play nine games against youth teams there as part of a two week soccer tour. Five years ago the American kids would have been better off spending their time collecting baseball cards rather than being subjected to devastation and demoralization. Not any more.

The Red Wings won seven of nine, shutting out five of their opponents. One of their two losses was to the youth team sponsored by the Netherland's best professional club, Ajax. The style of play was as important as the outcome, because the Red Wings showed a variety of techniques which baffled their opponents.

There is one little catch—a fair one—to the Red Wings' success—over a two year period they had played more than a hundred games together. Roughly a game a week. Of course, playing experience is what is needed for Americans to develop into good soccer players, and the Annandale team is an example of the results within reach.

The California Youth Soccer Association has made arrangements to allow its soccer players to have games year round. The Association proposed a split season for boys under nineteen. The youth season would be built around the high school season so it would not interfere with scholastic play, but would allow for league play before and after the high school season. The league season would end in time for players to play for the national youth team, Olympic team or other select teams if chosen.

Of course, soccer must be careful to avoid burn-out phenomenon which results in a youngster playing so much of a supervised sport at such an early age that he gets sick of it. First signs of this phenomenon are when the child misplaces his uniform, forgets where practice is, doesn't know if his team won or lost, or indicates he'd rather take a bath than talk about his game. A kid suffering from one or more of these symptoms should be given a rest. Let him skip a couple of practices, avoid talking about the sport, don't force him to try and strip the ball from you or block your shots on the goal. Soccer, like any other sport, can become a burden at an early age if overdone.

Naturally, susceptibility to the burn-out phenomenon will vary greatly according to a young person's age, skill, personal desire and other factors. But for the early teenager who has made a steady growth through various levels of play and who shows definite interest in playing soccer, 40 games per year spread evenly over a spring and fall season seems like enough time to develop skills without burning-out enjoyment.

Many soccer programs on the youth and scholastic levels are varying their competition, a good idea for sustaining competitiveness and encouraging skill development without having to force it. Many neighboring states have all-star games or, better yet, competition between individual teams from each state. Some fortunate teams like the Red Wings and the Milwaukee Soccer Club raise money or get sponsors to send them to compete overseas. Eaglebrook School in Deerfield, Mass. hosted the North East Junior School Soccer Tournament in 1974 with sixteen school teams from four states involving over 320 boys between the ages of ten and fifteen. The teams played a round robin tournament of twelve minute games, a good way to work on skills under fast-paced pressure situations.

In general, Steps 1 and 2 of the popularity progression are already well established across the U.S.A. as the youth leagues grow in numbers and members. However the higher up the progression the more fragmented soccer's following becomes. Again, this will vary in different parts of the country, but Steps 3 and 4 are only recently beginning to develop strength. Soccer is still a minor sport in many high schools in the country. But there are signs that the concept of the popularity progression will take hold at the high school level and boost the sport into prominence. It's already happening in some areas.

There are some 125,000 high school soccer players in the U.S., up from only 42,000 in 1967. Interest in high school soccer is often first expressed at the club level and then it moves into varsity competition. Soccer players find that the economics of the game makes points with athletic directors. Teams more concerned with playing than looking like fashion plates can outfit themselves with shorts, T-shirts and socks for $8-$12 per person, certainly not an unreasonable figure for most schools carrying a fifteen to eighteen man squad. Shoes, an investment of ten dollars plus, are purchased by individual players. Five balls, two good game balls and three for practice, total $100-$125. A coach, depending on the school system's policies, will vary in cost. Football fields and some baseballs fields convert easily into soccer fields, but because of scheduling conflicts and reseeding plans high school soccer players often find themsleves playing at odd times of the year, week, and day. Still, for approximately $1,500 (not including coaches pay, but including cost of officials, goals and miscellaneous items) a school can field a varsity soccer team and much of that money is a one-shot investment. The problem facing athletic directors, of course, is determining what, if any, revenue soccer can produce since replacing some uniforms and balls every year or two may be yet another burden on an already tight budget.

A little selling is frequently required to ease an athletic director's apprehensions. If a good community youth soccer program is operating it may hit the athletic director as a chance to snap up some future spectators if a good high school team is established. High schools on Long Island, where youth programs have been providing impetus, began attracting upwards of 750 spectators in

1974. Of course, the old high school willingness for an activity to become self-supporting by pestering family, friends, neighbors and relatives into buying light bulbs, foot long chocolate bars, gawdy stickers and assorted other items may result in enough phone calls to the school demanding an end to the huckstering that the sport winds up being subsidized.

Few names of schools known for collegiate soccer are considered important, or even known at all, to college football and basketball fans. Howard University (1975 NCAA soccer champ), St. Louis University (NCAA champs for ten of the last fifteen years), Quincy College, Hartwick College, and Brockport St. are some collegiate soccer heavyweights. But more and more schools known for their all around athletic programs are making their way into soccer competition. Pressure from student fans to field competitive soccer squads and the attractive economics of the sport have prompted larger schools like UCLA, Maryland University, Penn St. and others to strengthen their soccer programs.

According to Penn State's Walter Bahr, the colleges are slowly seeing results of soccer's impact on youth. "The caliber of play is improving every year," Bahr says, "because we're getting players who have had more exposure to soccer at an early age."

In keeping with his preference toward developing Americans, Bahr started ten American players on his 1974 team which went 8-1-3 for the season and earned a place in the nation's Top-20. In his recruiting for 1975, Bahr concentrated on four American born players and two naturalized citizens. Unfortunately, Bahr has only one and one quarter scholarships to spread around as an inducement to play soccer at Penn St.

Bert Grell of the Washington Diplomats shows good heading technique, complete with grimace. *Photo by Mark Rattner.*

Leroy Deleon of the Washington Diplomats shows the correct way to control and dribble a soccer ball — using the instep of the foot. He also demonstrates how to push in order to beat an opponent to the ball, a foul if the referee chooses to call it. *Photo by Mark Rattner.*

Though Penn St. soccer is played on Jeffrey Field (it does not have to share with the football team) and drew an average of 5,000 fans per game, there was no admission fee for the games which means soccer was a subsidy case. As such, it does not have an expansive budget.

"We had invitations to play in tournaments in Dallas, St. Louis, Florida and at Clemson in South Carolina," says Bahr, "but the cost prohibits it right now. Athletic directors are still football oriented, but soccer's making headway. We're increasing our schedule to fourteen games for 1975 and eventually I think we could get two games per week over a twelve week period."

Bahr is also thinking about charging admission to the games figuring a good mostly American team will draw paying students. The potential to draw paying crowds is certainly there since 3,500 seat Jeffrey Field packed in 6,500 for Army and 6,300 for Hartwick.

For smaller schools looking for a fall sport, but shying away from the wallet-wrecking expenses of American football, soccer is becoming a favorite. Eckard College in St. Petersburg, Fla. is a prime example. With an enrollment of less than a thousand students, Eckard entered into Division III soccer play in 1973. The school's baseball coach also had a New England soccer background, so he took on the soccer coaching duties as well. Despite the fact that the school offers no baseball or soccer scholarships, the coach looked for players interested in the chance to play two varsity sports. By 1974 Eckard was playing every major college in Florida in soccer and beating most of them.

Big schools with historically successful athletic programs that have been slow to develop their soccer programs already have a lot of catching up to do to compete with already strong soccer schools. A major problem soccer coaches at the larger schools face is the inability to say to a prospect, "If you go with us, the pros will be watching you" like their colleagues in football or basketball can. Because soccer has just reached the fringes of Step 7 in the popularity progression, the collegian, particularly the American soccer playing collegian, does not play his college soccer with an eye toward the pros, although approximately 25 percent of the NASL's 69 draft choices in 1975 wound up on the playing roster of one of the 20 teams at the start of the 1975 season. While 25 percent may seem high, it meant that only approximately 5 percent of all of the NASL players in 1975 came into the league as a result of the 1975 draft. Considering that the NASL's prime attraction to draft picks is not a way to make a living but a chance to play soccer in the U.S.A.'s most prestigious league, the NASL's ability to sign nearly 25 percent of its draftees is surprising.

"Some college players today get out of school and try the pros but after a couple of years they can't afford to go on," Walter Bahr says, offering a partial explanation. "That doesn't really help the colleges right now, and it's not helping for the pros to have eleven foreign players on the field most of the time either."

The pro teams with their low salaries and high percentage of foreign players might not be providing a lot of incentive to youth at present, bqt they're all watching with gleaming eyes as the steps of the popularity progression form. The overwhelming belief around the NASL is that soccer has established itself with youngsters around the country and the game will be reaping benefits in years to come.

"You can see seven, eight and nine year olds everywhere getting the skills of soccer," says Gordon Brown, coach of the New York Cosmos, better known as Pelé's team. "These will be the players who will make the game go in the U.S."

Even men without a Pelé to tinge their opinions put their faith in youth. "The first sign that the game is exploding is the number of kids playing it," says Philadelphia Atoms coach Al Miller. "It's still a new game in many areas, but it's catching on with kids everywhere."

Brown and Miller and the rest are not blindly optimistic. In and around the cities where NASL teams are located youth soccer leagues are thriving, a sure sign that the popularity progression theory is working. Around the Dallas metroplex, an estimated 50,000 youngsters play; around Washington, D.C., 50,000; around Seattle, Washington, 40,000; around St. Louis, 35,000; and so on around the NASL. The links are solid, forming rapidly. The growth of youth leagues across the country is soccer's strongest point as a sport in the U.S. today.

Soccer has reached the kids of suburbia and beyond. The crucial point will come when the kids of today become the potential stars of tomorrow and the pro teams try to lure them into the game. It will take more the the opportunity to watch foreigners play to keep the progression alive. When that point is reached, the pros must make a commitment to use primarily Americans on their teams or else soccer may kick itself right out of the old U.S.A.

Soccer is a difficult sport for a new American fan to get used to watching because so many people are unfamiliar with it. Whereas even a casual observer would know basically what to cheer or boo at a football, basketball or baseball game, the same people find themselves lost at soccer games. Unfortunately, there are a lot of soccer groupies—people who have had some association with soccer in the past—who attend games and fancy themselves as experts. The groupies know a few "laws" of the game, as rules are called, and a little of the technical side so they tend to intimidate the less informed.

No more! Soccer American style is fair game for anyone to mold to their own likes and dislikes. If the game wants to make it in America, then it must adjust to American cheers and catcalls. It's not a difficult game to enjoy, once you know what to look for.

Soccer, a game controlled by the rulings of essentially one man, the referee, lends itself to a lot of action away from the ball. Trips, pushes and holds are common away from the main action and they're worth watching from the fan's standpoint. Soccer can be a game of intimidation and frustration and the little battles going on when the referee's not looking frequently become important when the pressure's on. Of course, some of the contact, like charging, where players can make shoulder-to-shoulder contact, is allowed and it can definitely affect a player's performance.

The whole focus of fan attention is different in soccer, and it takes some getting used to. Most American sports revolve around the upper body. The focus in watching football is on the shoulders, forearms and helmet. In basketball, although the legs do the propelling, the result of that propulsion comes from the hands. In baseball, it's primarily the upper body—the arms and shoulders while swinging, the arms while throwing, the hands while fielding. Soccer, however, moves the focus of attention to the legs and feet. And when attention is shifted upward in soccer, it's usually to the higher points of the head.

The dribble in soccer is controlled with the inside of the foot. A good dribbler can run at full speed while keeping the ball well within his stride, using the physical power needed to run very fast but just tapping the ball with his foot. When the dribbler wants to elude a defender and change direction, he must do his faking with his legs and feet without losing control of the ball. Three things are really happening at once—the dribbler is controlling the ball, faking, and changing direction all with the same part of the body. There is no move in baseball, football or basketball which demands as much from one part of the body at the same time, because control of the ball in those sports comes primarily from the hands.

Soccer kicks are also supposed to be controlled by the inside of the foot, although more than a few overanxious players have booted the ball with the front of their feet. An experienced soccer player can put spin on

Clyde Best (left) and Brian Pillinger know that soccer action focuses on the feet. Here forward Best tries to get around defender Pillinger by changing the pace of his dribble. *Photo by John E. de Freitas.*

A soccer kick is taken with the inside of the foot, non-kicking leg braced, body tilted slightly back, arms spread and kicking leg swung through like a pendulum. *Photo by John E. de Freitas.*

his kicks to make them sail or bounce in odd directions. But the most enjoyable kick to watch is one taken straight on goal from 15 to 20 yards away. The attacking player keeps his non-kicking leg rigid, leans his body slightly back, generally spreads his arms for balance and swings his kicking leg through like a pendulum driving the inside of the foot through the center of the ball. A well executed kick is completed in a fraction of a second and is best compared to a swing in baseball where the body acts as a hinge and the arms and shoulders propel the bat through the ball. The result is the same in each case—hard, fast line drives.

The legal way to stop a good dribbler in soccer is by tackling, a term which is considerably different in soccer than in football although it often has the same result. Tackling in soccer means a defensive player uses his feet to try to take the ball from the offensive player. Naturally, errant swipes at the ball mean bruises and cuts on shins and ankles.

The slide tackle is one of soccer's most enjoyable plays from the spectator standpoint. Anyone who has marvelled at a baseball player who slides into a base and in the same motion pops to his feet will appreciate a slide tackle. Slide tackles frequently occur with both the dribbler and defender on the run. The defender slides into the path of the running dribbler and oh-so-daintily plucks the ball from him. It requires precise timing, not to mention the nerve involved in extending your leg in the way of a hard running opponent. Slide tackles have been known to send both dribbler and tackler sprawling.

While soccer fans must watch the legs and feet, they will see some of the most physically appealing action occurring around the head. The inclination to strike a soccer ball with the head comes from the gut. The ball, weighing between 14 and 16 ounces, comes hard and fast. A properly headed ball is struck with the center of the forehead with eyes open and mouth closed. A misjudged header hitting the face or top of the head means pain. Heading for direction frequently requires coordinating a jump, proper heading technique, body control and a twist of the neck. Good headers use the neck and head like a baseball player uses the wrist and hand. The wrist snaps the hand to provide force. In soccer, the neck snaps the head with much the same effect.

For the fan the appeal of watching a header comes largely from the vulnerability of the player, especially if more than one man is going for the ball. A misjudged header may result in the skull of one man being snapped into the skull of another, and there's no helmet to absorb that contact. Players attempting to head a ball often twist their necks into positions with enough force to put an improperly trained person in traction for weeks. Then, of course, there's the possibility of muffing a header altogether, where the ball flies over the player's head and he's left snapping his head at thin air.

Every sport has its glamour position — the basketball center, the baseball pitcher, the football quarterback — and in soccer it's the goalkeeper. He may also be called the goalie and some groupies prefer calling him just the "keeper", but that's reason enough not to use that term. In any case, he's the man who must react under intense pressure which is generally obvious to everyone in the crowd. He wears a different color jersey for identification and gloves for protection. His job description is simple — stop the ball from going into the net or pack up and get out of town quick.

He's susceptible to some of the fiercest contact in the game since players tend to act slightly crazed in front of the goal. The goalie must be willing to throw himself at a ball and smother it even though the attacker is in full kick. Sometimes a goalie must stretch his body to reach for a ball in the middle of a crowd of goal hungry opponents, leaving his ribs as unprotected targets for overzealous types.

The goalie must be acrobat, leader and quarterback every game. After making a save he must put the ball back into play for his teammates by kicking or passing it. Professional goalies can punt 50-70 yards regularly, accurately sending the ball to teammates downfield. They must be able to throw long pinpoint passes to catch a sleeping defense off guard. And the goalkeeper must be able to direct his team's defensive play when opponents are applying pressure on offense.

But most of all, the goalie must be able to react to speeding shots coming with strange spins from odd angles out of crowds of players. He must decide to catch, smother, punch, kick, block or tip the ball away in an instant. Everyone expects him to succeed; when he fails, every person in the crowd sees it.

The interesting thing to notice about soccer players other than the goalkeeper is that regardless of their position they must have well-rounded skills. The four defenders who usually play from in front of the goalie to midfield, depending on the position of the ball, rarely get a chance to score but they still need well developed dribbling and kicking skills to move the ball from their end of the field to the offensive players. The three midfielders that most teams use must have highly developed scoring skills, to help out on an offensive push,

The slide tackle frequently sends both the offensive and defensive players sprawling. *Photo by Dennis Mallon.*

Dave D'Errico of the Seattle Sounders going downfield against the Washington Diplomats. *Photo by Steve Hammond.*

Soccer action occurs in bursts, demanding well timed passes, speed and quick reactions. *Photos by Dennis Mallon.*

and defensive skills, for dropping back to help stop an attack. Forwards, and most teams use three, get the most scoring glamour and they are generally the fastest sprinting and best scoring players. But the forwards must know how to tackle too, so when the opposing defense thwarts their attack the forwards can take the ball back quickly and keep the pressure on.

Soccer is played on a field measuring from 100 to 130 yards long and 50 to 100 yards wide, with end lines called goal lines and sidelines called sidelines. It's a large field and soccer players playing both 45 minute halves of non-stop running time will run from seven to twelve miles per game. The more things a player can do with the ball and the more moves he can make without it, the more valuable he is to his team.

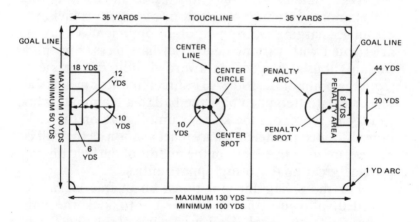

Naturally, soccer players become most intense in front of the goal, and action around the goal is often affected by two of soccer's more important rules — the awarding of goal and corner kicks. When the ball is in the vicinity of the goal line, defending teams under pressure sometimes find it wise to kick the ball over the goal line and out of bounds to avoid giving up a goal. The problem is that the attacking team is then awarded a corner kick, which means it puts the ball into play by kicking it from the corner on the defending team's end of the field. Corner kicks are valuable to the attacking team because they allow it to center the ball to a forward or some other target man breaking for the goal. Such commotion around the goal mouth is a goalkeeper's nightmare.

On the other hand, if the defense can cause the offense to lose the ball over the goal line, then the defending team is awarded a goal kick. The goalie can then boot the ball to some nice safe spot far away from the goal area.

When intense soccer action results in handling the ball, jumping into an opponent, or overzealous kicking, pushing, charging or tripping of an opponent, violators are treated with varying degrees of harshness. For mild fouling, abused players are awarded indirect free kicks from the point of the foul. An indirect free kick means the kicker must attempt to pass the ball to a teammate who can try to score, but the kicker cannot score on the kick himself. Since the defense may react as soon as the ball is kicked, indirect free kicks in the middle of the field do not provide great goal scoring opportunities.

For more flagrant violations, direct free kicks are awarded, allowing the kicker to try to kick the ball directly into the goal. However, since the defense can form a wall ten yards away from the ball, direct free kicks are not always easy scoring opportunities either, especially in midfield.

Penalty kicks provide the greatest opportunity to

score as the result of being fouled. They are awarded when an offensive players is violently fouled within the penalty area which extends 18 yards deep onto the field from the goal line and 44 yards wide around the goal. The offensive player kicks from the penalty mark which is located 12 yards directly in front of the goal. It's just the kicker and goalkeeper and it provides great one-on-one drama.

While free kicks are not the scoring threat that a penalty kick is, they are valuable in putting continued stress on the defense. They force the defense to stop for a moment while the offense makes its move. The move does not always result in a goal, but it disrupts the rhythm of the defensive team. A team that gives up a lot of corner kicks and free kicks is a team putting pressure on itself.

Soccer is, above all, a game of pressure, pacing and bursts. A team needs all three to win. If you see your favorites bombarding their opponents with shots, the inclination is to feel that eventually they'll start going in. But unless your team is in extremely good physical condition, or unless the opponents do not set up a ring of defenders around the goal, the physical drain on the aggressors will surely take its toll. The opposition needs only one or two well timed bursts to defeat a fatigued team.

Because of the physical demands, most teams try to set up their opponents and this is the time of the game that soccer knockers call boring. But it holds the same kind of excitement as watching a wide receiver set up a cornerback during a football game, or waiting for a mismatch in basketball, or seeing a pitcher set up a batter with a high hard one so he can sneak a third strike low and away. The team can't be bursting all the time in soccer, so it tries to catch its opponent off guard. The midfielders dribble leisurely and pass to one another, but one of the forwards is setting up his defender, throwing juke steps and fakes until suddenly he's racing toward the goal and his teammate with the ball must act immediately with a direct, accurate pass. Most of the time it does not result in a goal. But it's the repeated bursts of pressure, the setting up that will eventually cause a defense to break down and give up a score.

Scoring a goal in soccer is the result of such carefully timed maneuvers and such long arduous labor that the infrequent goals are usually wildly celebrated by players and fans alike. To the unobservant spectator, scoring in soccer appears haphazard and lucky, happening so unexpectedly that the drama is sometimes lost. To the more educated spectator, however, who allows himself to become involved in the intricacies of the game and who knows where to look for the pulse of the aciton, a goal in soccer is appreciated as the reward for carefully planned teamwork and individual skill. Much of the tension and temper flare-ups in soccer stem from the frustration involved in trying to score. It's difficult to accept that such concentration and effort may result in no goals, or, on a good day, two or three goals. Yet that is the essence of soccer — bursts of action all over the field designed to put stress on an opponent and precisely timed to result in a goal scored.

Pro soccer games in the U.S. are also puncuated by odd sounds. Players call to one another in an assortment of languages which are often better understood by opponents and teammates. Coaches frequently refer to their players as "lads," when their British is showing. Referees are called "referee" more often than "ref" even in heated situations. Few cheers used for American sports fit in soccer. Even "Block that kick!" from football is out of place because the ball changes possession so frequently.

Groupies have adopted some of the foreign sounding terms, feeling a sense of being "in" by shouting, "Come on, lads!" or "What's wrong with the bloody referee?" from the stands. Nothing says that fans in America can't roll out their old favorite sports terms for soccer — so call the players bums, or guys, or clowns, or sweethearts and by all means shout "ref" instead of referee, and stay away from the "bloody," it's so awfully British, you know.

Don't worry about using the classic soccer terms like calling a soccer field a "pitch" as the traditionalists do. In the U.S. it's a field, and that term will do just fine. the same goes for calling a team a "side" and a game a "match." There are football teams, baseball teams, basketball teams and soccer will be known by its teams too, and they'll play their games on our fields. And if we find it easier to say that a player is being guarded by an opponent instead of being "marked" by him, then guarded it will have to be. Let the traditionalists cringe. It's time to stop talking about soccer becoming an American game; it's time to start treating it like one.

To enjoy soccer, watch for mounting pressure, individual and team bursts of action, and maneuvers away from the ball. To enjoy it American style, get into it like you would any sport and forget about the groupies.

Two heads going after the same ball often results in body contact from the head on down. *Photo by Dennis Mallon.*

10.　　　When Will Soccer Really Score?

Soccer will not replace American football. It will not survive at the expense of baseball. The indoor game will not knock basketball and hockey out of the winter sports picture. Soccer will not replace any of the professional sports currently popular in the United States.

Soccer will survive as a sport on its own merits, drawing its own fans who will see it as *another* spectator sport but not necessarily the *only* one. By the early 1980s soccer should be a legitimate professional sport in the U.S. with American players earning salaries high enough to live on, and followed by knowledgeable American fans.

But it is not a guaranteed success.

Soccer has been incredibly fortunate in the success it has had since 1969. Despite folding franchises, part time players, lack of fan identification and some shaky management, soccer in the NASL has established itself as a force of the future in the sports world. The NASL interested national TV in at least a few games and the league has become the symbol of professionalism to the young. Soccer is becoming a respected American sport not just in the cities of the U.S., but in the suburbs and small towns of the country where identification is so important. But the game is at the put-up or shut-up stage of existence. It's made big noises, cried at being neglected, touted itself to all who would listen and many who would not. Pelé, big crowds in the west, TV, and strong interest among youth have turned heads in soccer's direction. If it wants to move in with the heavyweights, it must move now. There are several key areas to watch as soccer makes its move.

● The NASL Office — There are strong commitments to pro soccer today. The league office could be stronger in its push for Americanization, but at least it has made the NASL known as the major pro soccer body in the eyes of the general public. As the center of U.S. soccer, the league appears strong and stable.

When Phil Woosnam's days as commissioner are up, soccer will have him to thank for patiently laying the framework of a strong pro league, at least symbolically. Where the NASL has become known from 1969-1975, Woosnam has had something to do with it. Woosnam cautiously makes ten years the length of time it will take before soccer becomes a major sport. As usual, he arrives at the figure through a plan.

"We must have a youngster and a pro image. The media will watch our growth very carefully and as we grow they'll write about different levels of the sport. It will become a pipeline as youngsters gain allegiance to the sport and go to the top.

"Soccer is a cheap sport. It gives good value for the money. Our ticket prices are not at the same high level as other sports. As more youngsters play, TV sponsors will become interested."

All this, Woosnam feels, will make soccer irresistable. And he's probably right. But in one of the oddities of success, as the sport that Woosnam so

A spectacular save! *Photo by Mark Rattner.*

carefully nurtured grows, he becomes less the center of power and more reliant upon the wishes of the owners. Woosnam's direct force is weakening as his league grows stronger. How Woosnam changes as his role changes is important to soccer's future and to his future as commissioner.

• Individual Clubs Around the NASL — Stability has been, is, and will continue to be an important word in pro soccer's drive for acceptability because soccer cannot afford a breakdown in confidence. While the NASL has achieved recognition and confidence as a whole, it still needs some work on individual club levels. Roster, management, and stadium changes are plentiful each year. In midseason coaches are still flying off to faraway places for a new player or two to add to the roster. Final rosters do not have to be completed until July 25, just one month before the end of the season. Media relations personnel for some teams are replaced annually, before any meaningful rapport with the media can be established.

Teams must start making commitments to players and office personnel so a sense of belonging is built on the club. If foreign players must be used, they should be only very high quality players and American teams should not purchase them on a loan basis. Instead, the clubs should move the player to America and help find him a year round job in the states. If foreign talent must be raided, it should be an all-out raid so the players become part of the American communities.

• Use of American Players — Soccer clubs should adopt a rule by 1976 which says at least seven American players must be on the roster of each team; the Canadian franchises should have at least seven Canadians.

By 1977 all teams should be required to have at least six American players in the game at all times. The five remaining players can be foreigners, but preferably foreigners living in the U.S. year round.

By the start of the 1978 season, no foreigner on the roster of a United States team should be allowed to play for any other team in the world, except for their own national team. Elimination of loan players will force foreign players to decide where they can make the best deal for themselves and commit themselves to that team.

• Professional Status of Players — This is certainly one of the stickiest areas to watch since, in the area of salaries, teams can only be pushed so far before permanent bankruptcy threatens. But club owners willing to act quickly may still find that players' demands are not in the unreasonable stage yet. Insurance, retirement, more playing time for Americans, a total maximum salary limit paid to loan players before their elimination in 1978, a standard minimum starting salary for each new American player paid throughout the actual season, and compensation for attending off season training sessions are all areas in which owners could initiate action to appease players until revenue grows to allow higher salaries.

Traditionally, management does not like to part with its money since the green stuff has a way of making people extremely possessive. However, soccer club owners cannot afford *not* to raise salaries just as soon as possible because the magic carpet ride the sport has received in its semi-pro state won't last much longer. Owners can buy some time, but when loan players disappear, salaries should start rising.

• The National Team — Developing a successful

national team is also extremely important to pro soccer's fan appeal in the next decade or so. Soccer is a world game. If the U.S. fails to make a strong showing in either of the next two World Cups, American soccer will not receive the kind of impetus and attention international success brings.

As young United States talent comes up through the ranks, some incentives must be provided to encourage their participation on the national team. If it means giving national team players $10,000 bonuses immediately to encourage American players to make the team and attend regular practices, then start paying the money. The NASL and the USSF should get together and decide on a definite course of action based on real incentives to develop a strong national team.

• Expansion — As soccer searches for suitable locations, it tends to look toward already established sports towns. Lamar Hunt says he would like to see the league grow to 24 cities eventually, including "Montreal, Detroit, Atlanta and a fourth city from Cleveland, Pittsburgh, Houston and New Orleans. Detroit is a big advertising center and Atlanta would put us in the mid south. Two of the other cities would put us in most of the major cities."

While such expansion plans sound sensible enough, the NASL should take one major precaution — do not locate in the same ballpark as the city's baseball team. Put the new franchises in smaller, suburban stadiums for the first few years. Even cities with the lowliest of baseball teams have allegiances to them and summertime soccer cannot count on drawing fans away from baseball.

• The American Soccer League — The NASL should move to join forces with ASL cities to form a farm

Leroy Deleon dribbling downfield. *Photo by John E. de Freitas.*

system comprised of current ASL teams. The ASL does not have any real hope at this time of competing with the NASL for national recognition. While the ASL has been around longer, its operations are not of the same magnitude as the NASL's. By joining with the NASL in a farm league capacity, both leagues would benefit. The advantage to the NASL would be the opportunity to train young players. For the ASL, successful franchises would be prime candidates for expansion sites in the future. In addition to regular farm league play, the ASL teams could play exhibitions against local college and amateur teams.

• Identity — Soccer is a new sport to the U.S. It should work on developing itself around its newness. It has taken soccer three quarters of a century to break out of its city niches and now it should capitalize on its escape. Soccer should become a sport for suburbia since that's where much of its appeal lies among the youth.

New relationships with fans have developed in many cities, relationships based on informality. Not that every club should sing to its fans or hand out flowers for every game, because then the novelty would soon wear off. But ideas like that set up a different personality for the sport and they should be encouraged.

Soccer traditionalists should stop niggling over proposed changes in the rules of the game. Americans like a little contact, so don't scream about losing finesse everytime a referee overlooks a shove or two. For that matter, let's take the referees out of those incredibly square looking black shorts and black shirts with white collars and cuffs.

And drop the pitch that soccer is the "real" football.

Americans don't want to hear it. In the U.S.A., soccer is soccer and football is football.

There is an air of confidence about soccer in the U.S.A. today that is encouraging for the sport. It's a confidence that indicates the weaknesses are known and will be dealt with.

"Soccer is doing very well indeed," says John Best, coach of the Seattle Sounders. "When will it succeed? It has succeeded, there's no doubt about it. The only problem is that it hasn't completely succeeded in our league so people don't realize the ground swell soccer has. You can see growth, not only in attendance numbers, but the standard of play among older boys. When it really gets into the college program, watch out.

"The league's level of play is improving greatly too. The game is opening up, and I support that idea. This is a young enough league to experiment with some rules changes.

"American players are improving. We coaches need to work patiently with them, but there's a lot of individual talent.

"Economics is a key area for soccer. In 1969 when we almost collapsed, everything was cut to the bone and gradually things have improved. People are just starting to see some monetary benefits and they'll be upgraded as our income increases. We'll have the opportunity to build more and more benefits as time goes by. It's people just beyond us who will really receive the benefits."

Lamar Hunt, like John Best, experienced the mistakes and failures of pro soccer in the late sixties. Yet he hasn't given up on the game and he feels it will begin paying off soon.

"Today it's hard to realize how far down and bad things were in the early days of the league," Hunt says. "But now the vital signs are all there. It's no longer a question of whether soccer will happen, but when it will happen.

"Some teams will finish in the black for the first time this year (1975). Teams are nothing but businesses and they need to see the chance to make a profit in order to keep going. We're quite a ways from making a profit here in Dallas because the team has been a disappointment. We're not one of the bright spots in the league. But I'm going to stay with the sport.

"Soccer will make it, perhaps it will be in different years in different cities. Within ten years the sport will be nationally accepted. In some cities it may be earlier than in others."

It will be a while before the accuracy of Hunt's prediction can be seen and while he won't go broke waiting, others might. It's going to be an interesting decade for soccer, one that will see many pro teams either vanish or flourish. While the game will be hindered by some internal problems of economics and direction, it will be helped by the steady elimination of the foreign stigma.

Soccer is the immigrant sport. It's done its time in the confines of the cities and mining towns. It stuck to its own kind for years, entertaining those who knew it, enduring the snubs of those who didn't. It tried to force itself on Americans before they were ready for it and was rejected, so the game made friends among the young who are not bound by prejudices. The kids took it home with them, integrated it with time spent playing status sports, introduced it to their parents. And now soccer finds itself being accepted because it can do the things that make Americans most proud.

It *can* make money. It *can* support itself. It *can* entertain. It *can* develop people physically. *It can even make the U.S. respected around the world.*

Yes, soccer is becoming American in the most American of ways — by starting out as foreign and gradually making a place for itself. That's the way the U.S. is supposed to work, and many of the men with foreign birthplaces who helped establish the game here are completely caught up in soccer Americana now.

"I don't like to hear soccer classified as an ethnic game," says Dennis Viollet in a British accent somewhat modified by his years in the States as he reflects on the game in America. "You see, I don't want to feel like an outcast or that the game is an outcast. Soccer has a future in this country. Soccer belongs in the United States . . . and so do I."

Pelé, at 34 years old, is still an elusive man to cover one-to-one. *Photo by Dennis Mallon.*